Walter Chalmers Smith

Hilda among the broken Gods

Walter Chalmers Smith

Hilda among the broken Gods

ISBN/EAN: 9783337138875

Printed in Europe, USA, Canada, Australia, Japan

Cover: Foto ©ninafisch / pixelio.de

More available books at **www.hansebooks.com**

HILDA AMONG THE BROKEN GODS.

PUBLISHED BY
JAMES MACLEHOSE, GLASGOW.

MACMILLAN AND CO., LONDON.

London,	Hamilton Adams and Co.
Cambridge,	Macmillan and Co.
Edinburgh,	Douglas and Foulis.

HILDA

AMONG THE BROKEN GODS

BY THE AUTHOR OF "OLRIG GRANGE"

Glasgow
JAMES MACLEHOSE
PUBLISHER TO THE UNIVERSITY
1878

All rights reserved

To

Theodore Martin, C.B.

I HAVE no "Shootings in the Highlands,"
  Nor house in some "Marine Parade,"
Nor yacht to sail 'mong sunny islands,
With prow low-rippling through the silence
  Of quiet waters deep-embayed.

And yet when Autumn tints the woods,
  I have my little pleasure-trip
Among the haunted solitudes
Where Silence on Parnassus broods,
  With hushing finger on her lip.

It costs me neither railway fare,
   Nor bill for tailor or for draper,
Nor rent of summer lodgings bare;
I get my little change of air
   For nothing but some pens and paper.

And there I make from day to day
   The world I live in—hill and dale,
And seas where slimy monsters play,
And sunny glades, and gardens gay,
   The haunt of thrush and nightingale.

Alone, I muse by fern-fringed rill,
   Or hold discourse with wives and yeomen,
Or dainty maidens moping still
For fantasy; and at my will
   They come and go, my men and women.

Last autumn, somehow—for there's law
   Controlling even a world so plastic—
On every picture that I saw
There fell a shade of gloom and awe
   From solemn pile Ecclesiastic;

DEDICATION.

From tottering steeple, falling cross,
   From storied window rudely shattered,
From nave and chancel suffering loss,
From priest and people as they toss
   The creeds about in fragments tattered.

And now I bring my autumn booty
   Spoil of the sunny hours, to thee
Who gave'st an English tongue to Goethe,
To Heine's wit, Catullus' beauty,
   And sympathy and help to me.—

But a slight offering, nothing more
   Than you shall get from lark or linnet,
Or homely sparrow at the door—
A song which from the heart I pour,
   It's only worth the heart that's in it.

CONTENTS.

	PAGE
PROLOGUE,	1

Book First.

CLAUD MAXWELL, POET, ... 7

Book Second.

HILDA, SAINT-WIFE, ... 51

Book Third.

WINIFRED URQUHART, MATERIALIST, . 125

Book Fourth.

LUKE SPROTT, EVANGELIST, . . 161

Book Fifth.

REV. ELPHINSTONE BELL, PRIEST, . 203

EPILOGUE, ... 240

L'ENVOI, . 245

Hilda among the Broken Gods.

Prologue.

IT is a Church of the Ages, all
    Arched and pillared and grandly towered,
With many a niche on the buttressed wall,
    And delicate tracery, scrolled and flowered:
Gargoyles gape, and arches fly
From base to base of the pinnacles high,
And the great cross points to the solemn sky.

A stately Church, and a Church all through,
    Everywhere shaped by a thought divine,
With symbols of Him who is Just and True,
    And emblems of Him who is Bread and Wine,
It is dowered with wealth of land and gold,
And memories high of the days of old,
And of sheep that were lost gathered into its fold.

Lord bishops sleep their slumber deep
   Under mitre and crosier carved in stone;
There are brasses quaint for the warrior saint
   Who had battled at Acre and Ascalon;
In the low-groined crypts lie kings and earls,
Resting now from their plots and quarrels,
But they mix not their dust with the rustic carles.

It is not day, and it is not dark,
   And the altar-lights are burning dim;
One sings, but it is not priest nor clerk,
   And he chaunts no psalm, and he sings no hymn.
Who are these that are trooping in,
With grimy visage, and bearded chin,
Rude and unmannered, with noisy din?

Some one is wailing—a poor soul ailing
   Down in the dim aisles far away;
Who is that droning? is he intoning
   The great Athanasian curse to-day?
Silence that chatter and laughter there,
And do not stand bonneted up to stare—
Hush! that is surely the voice of prayer.

First Voice.

They have made thy Temple a place abhorred,
    They have mocked thy Christ, for his own betrayed him;
And now they have taken away my Lord,
    Ah woe! and I know not where they have laid him.

Second Voice.

Now that the gods are certainly dead—
    Brahmâ and Zeus and the Father, and all—
With a desk and a lime-light overhead,
    We might use this up for a lecture-hall.
We could shew them things on the altar there—
    Bringing the light to the proper focus—
Wonderful transformations rare,
    Would beat the priests with their hocus-pocus:
With two or three chemicals we could make
    Nature her miracle-power surrender,
And a glass, at the angle fit, would wake
    As gruesome a ghost as the witch of Endor.
Everything here would give point to my hits
At the monk's huge faith, and his little wits,
As I drive at Bigots, and shout for Truth,
And laugh at the dreams of the world's raw youth.

Third Voice.

A pest on all the reforming crew,
Savant or Puritan, old or new!
See how the rogues come tramping in,
Now that they have not to praise or pray—
Faugh! what a breath of tobacco and gin!
They crowd to church because God is away!
And they've smashed that pitying angel's face,
That touched one's heart with a tender grace,
The best of their brute-wits could never replace.
If there be angels good or bad,
I very much doubt, and I do not much care;
But yet what a pitying look it had,
Beaming down from the oriel there!
Will no one silence that idiot's chatter
About laws, forsooth, of health and riches?
I'd rather the old priest's "stabat-mater"—
If we had but the ordeal now for witches,
Wouldn't I souse him into the water!

Fourth Voice.

Anathema Maranatha! Hark!
Be he sinner or be he saint,

There is no place in the saving Ark
For one who keeps but a cobweb faint
Of doubt in his heart, or doubt in his head,
About any one article I have read.
"Credo," that is the key of heaven;
The more incredible, so much more
Virtue lies in the Credo given
To open the everlasting door.
Thurifer, let the censer wave:
"Hoc est corpus," lift it high;
Christ is risen from the stone-sealed grave;
Now let us forth with him, and die
Into the life that comes thereby.
In high procession the priests will go
Chaunting the *Dies Irae* low,
Dies illa, sad and slow.
So the Church in the days of old,
Robed in linen and purple and gold,
Foiled the Devil, and all his tricks,
And drove out the swine with a crucifix.

FIRST VOICE (*far away*).

They have taken away my Lord,
And I know not where they have laid him!

So it went wailing down the long aisle,
   Mixed with the hum of the priest and the people;
And a shudder passed through the massive pile,
   From the low-groined crypt to the cross on the steeple:
And the glimmering lights on the altar died,
No more the priest-hymn sobbed and sighed,
But a hollow wind wailed through the transept wide.

BOOK FIRST.

Claud Maxwell, Poet.

I DO not blame thee, Hilda; did not blame thee even then
  When all my life fell dark, and all my way was hard to see;
And when I drifted, aimless, among clear-purposed men,
  Though often wroth at myself, yet I could never be wroth with thee.

Where art thou, where, my darling? for thou art my darling still,
  So gladsome and so winsome, and in beauty so complete!
The old home is as you left it, waiting for my love to fill
  Her corner by the fireside, or the sunny window seat.

But nevermore thou comest, though evermore I go
  Where thoughts of thee shall meet me as a sure-
    returning pain;
I cannot keep from that which only keeps alive
    my woe,
  And I would not keep from it until thou comest
    back again.

Lonely now the old familiar walks beside the
    brattling brooks,
  And lone with awful silence are the evening
    hours I sit;
I think I should go mad, but for the trick of
    writing books,
  Though I care but for the writing, not for that
    which I have writ.

Dead is all the old ambition; dead the heart to
    lettered fame,
  Though the humour have its pranks yet, and the
    fancy will have play;
I heed not for the Public praise, nor for the Critic's
    blame,
  Nor for the larger shadow that I cast upon my
    way.

O my rose was only budding when I laid it on
    my breast,
  And I watched the leaves unfolding, and the
    tender blushes flit;
Now my rose is broke and withered—and I broke
    it whom it blest—
  Yet the fragrance haunts my life still, and is all
    that sweetens it.

No, I do not blame you, Hilda; we were both of
    us so young,
  And I had a peremptory way, ungracious, unbe-
    seeming,
And a petulant hot humour, and an often silent
    tongue
  Which you thought betokened anger when my
    mind was only dreaming.

But I had no right to dream when I was called
    to play the man,
  And to cherish, with fond love, the love that put
    its trust in me:
Better lose the wayward Artist in the drudging Artisan
  Than take the yoke of love, and live as free among
    the free.

And doubtful shadows come and go, and we, of noth-
    ing sure,
  Have yet no qualms in trifling with a tranquil faith
    and true!
Ay me! it was her quiet faith that made her heart so
    pure,
  Yet I troubled its calm waters with the wanton
    stones I threw.

But O I loved you, Hilda, and will love you ever-
    more;
  I cannot chose but love you, be the anguish
    what it will,
For the very pain of loving is all other joys before:
  Though you broke my heart in pieces, every bit
    would love you still.

Though you broke my heart in pieces, I would
    love you more than all
  Who might seek to bind it up again; for love
    alone can bind
What only love can break; and all the fragments
    broken small
  Would but glass as many Hildas in the mirror
    of my mind.

What memories gather round me, sitting by the lonely hearth!
  They will not leave the house, those flitting ghosts of other days;—
Here a whispering, there a rustling, or an echo of old mirth,
  Or a face out of the darkness with a sad, rebuking gaze.

Ah me, but to remember how I placed you with your back
  Against the old wych-elm tree in the golden summer tide,
As we went, with slate and satchel, down the dim, green Lovers' Walk,
  And half in fear, and half in jest, you vowed to be my bride!

But with me it was right earnest; I exulted from that day
  That mine thou wert, and mine alone, and ever must be mine;
And I played protector grandly if our schoolmates in their play
  Did but touch thy finger roughly, or lift their eyes to thine.

O had we ne'er as children played together in the street,
  Never waded in the burns, nor plaited rushes on the lea,
Never busked us with the blue bells, never chanced on earth to meet,
  Till we looked upon each other when our Love had eyes to see!

For cousinship will hardly grow to perfect wedded love;
  There lacks the charm of wonder, and the mystery of fear;
It fits too easy on us, like a worn, familiar glove,
  And we tend it not so nicely, though we hold it all as dear.

I cannot but remember—we were still but girl and boy—
  That night we went to buy the ring, how fain we were to linger,
Half-afraid and half-ashamed to ask about the mystic toy,
  And how they all slipped loosely up and down the taper-finger.

Then our cottage, and the garden with the sea-
  pink borders! Now,
 I bethink me, we came to it ere the apple-blossom
  fell,
And the bloom was on our love as the bloom was
  on the bough,
 And there was singing in the trees, and in our
  hearts as well—

Singing of our happy fancies, singing of our joyous
  hopes!
 All our life was filled with singing, as the skylark
  fills the sky:
O the music of that gladness, in our hearts and
  in the copse,
 Swelling with a tender sweetness, and the peace
  that came thereby!

Then, the lengthening summer twilights, as we
  looked down on the river
 Gleaming silvery in the shallows, glooming darkly
  in the pools!
And the silent, sleepy village, with its blue smoke
  curling ever—
 Welcome sight to weary labour plodding home-
  ward with its tools!

And the tall green cones of poplar that around the
    kirkyard stood,
  And the gilded weather-cock that flashed the
    sunlight from the spire,
And the red glow on the window panes; and then
    the quiet mood
  That came on with the stars, and drew us
    closer to the fire!

I would not but remember those welcome, winsome
    hours
  That crowned the day's fit labour with fit recom-
    pence of rest,
And how we watched the laden bees amid the
    honeyed flowers:
  Yet I hardly seemed at home in life, but some-
    how like a guest.

There was a feeling haunted me, that all might be
    untrue—
  An unreal, phantom idyll—an illusion of the
    brain;
It did not look like fact, but like a dream that
    only knew
  The lawlessness of Fancy, and had banished
    grief and pain.

So passed in tender bliss the weeks and months
of love and peace,
And I wondered when I should awake, and find
the dream was gone;
So passed the year and day, and still the wonder
did not cease,
Although there came a frustrate hope that left
us still alone.

So passed the time in services of love and patient
duty,
And there was no cloud of trouble, and no fret
of wearing strife;
And still its memories cling to me, and clothe
with dreams of beauty,
As with ivy green and wallflower, the dim ruin
of my life.

For it is a dim, grey ruin where no cheerful work
is done,
Nor sound of gladness heard, but only moaning
of the wind,
And lonely desolation sits aweary of the sun,
With little caring for myself, and little for my
kind.

I know that that is wrong; that it is weak to yield
    to it;
  That manhood has its duty even when life is
    cold and grey—
Duty never half so noble, nor so strengthening and
    fit,
  As when the clouds have gathered thick, and
    darkened all the day.

I plead not for myself; I know that I am weak
    and poor,
  A creature of the sunshine, and my sunshine was
    so brief:
I have no heart to struggle now; I only can
    endure,
  And let the tide sweep on, as I sit clinging to
    my grief.

What was it, first, that broke the spell, and showed
    that we were twain—
  United, and yet sundered by a strain of char-
    acter?
A trifle, yet it smote me with a disappointing pain
  Sharper than a grief more real, for it marred my
    thought of her.

I had a fond ambition, and she did not share
   in it;
  I thought to make her famous, and she did not
   care for fame;
And I often sat a-dreaming, and watched the
   moonbeams flit
  With the river flickering through them, and its
   ripple all aflame.

Bit from days of early childhood with the love of
   rhythmic song,
  I had yet a curious shame for that which was
   my secret pride,
And would hide my work in midnight, as if doing
   something wrong,
  Though I hoped the world would yet admire the
   thing I strove to hide.

How I covered reams of paper! how I treasured
   every scrap!
  I might outgrow the fancy, yet was loath to let
   it go:
How I watched the moods of Nature, as I lay
   upon her lap,
  And she spoke to me by flowers and birds, and
   streams that murmured low!

The winter and the summer and the morning and
    the night,
  All seasons and all creatures brought her mes-
    sages to me;
I loved the very newt that crawled among the
    lilies bright,
  And the tiger-branded wasp, and the drowsy
    yellow bee.

And the silence of the mountains spoke unutter-
    able things;
  And the sounding of the ocean was as silence
    in my soul;
And close to me, and conscious, lying warm as
    brooding wings,
  Lay the Mystery of mysteries that quickeneth the
    whole.

I was glancing only lately at those stiff and futile
    rhymes,
  Where half-formed thought was struggling for the
    forms of perfect Art,
And thinking how I treasured them, and read them
    many times;
  And even then to burn them, somehow went
    against my heart.

Poor stuff they are enow—a drift of dry and
    shrivelled weed,
  Marking where once the tide of froth and flying
    scud had been;
Yet will I keep this fragment, for scrawled on it I read,
  "My husband's nicest verses, though I scarce
    know what they mean:—"

Contrasts.

Twain are they, sundered each from each,
  Though oft together they are brought;
Discoursing in a common speech,
  Yet having scarce a common thought;
The same sun warmed them all their days,
  They breathe one air of life serene;
Yet, moving on their several ways,
  They walk with a whole world between.

I think they never meet without
  Some sharp encounter of their wits;
And neither hints a faith or doubt,
  The other does not take to bits;
For what the one regards with awe,
  The other holds a creed outworn;
And what this boasts as perfect law,
  That turns to laughter with his scorn.

No envious grudge is in their hearts,
  Detracting from the honour due
To nobler worth, or greater parts,
  Or larger grasp, or clearer view:
Simply there is a gulf between
  Their ways of life, and modes of thought,
And nothing is by either seen
  But as the other likes it not.

With vision keen and thought complete
  Cool-headed Warham holds his way,
And all that lies about his feet
  He makes it his, and clear as day;
All common things of natural birth
  He sets forth in a novel sense;
But never leaves the common earth
  To seek the dim Omnipotence.

He gathers knowledge hour by hour,
  Forgetting nought that once he knew,
And handling it with conscious power
  As matter certified and true;
And all he knows gives added might
  That still with harder thought combines;
We wonder at the shining light,
  He wonders less the more it shines!

He has slight pity for our pain,
   For weakness, he has none at all;
He is not proud, he is not vain;
   He is not either great or small;
But he is strong and hard and clear
   As is a frosty winter day,
And never sheds an idle tear,
   Nor flings an idle word away.

He cannot breathe but in the breath
   Of certainty and knowledge clear;
And where we have to walk by Faith
   He will not go; or will not fear
To search into the mysteries,
   And bid the haunting shadows go;
And yet, with all he knows and sees,
   True wisdom somehow does not grow.

But Cromer is of finer make,
   And doth with subtler thoughts commune—
Thoughts singing oft in dim daybreak,
   And silent oft in blaze of noon;
He sees the process Warham saw,
   But to the Power he is not blind,
Beholds the working of the Law,
   And bows to that which lies behind.

Seeking what knife can ne'er dissect,
  Nor flame-wrapt blowpipe can set free,
Nor chemic test can e'er detect,
  But only kindred mind can see,
He finds in everything a light
  Which, shunning finest power of sense,
Does more to make a man of might
  Than knowledge of the Why or Whence.

And much he knows, and much he thinks,
  But he *is* more than all he knows;
For still aspiring, still he drinks
  Fresh inspiration as he goes,
More careful that the man should grow
  Than that the mind should understand:
He loves all creatures here below,
  And touches all with tender hand.

He pities all the pained and weak,
  And feels for their unhappy fate;
Simple and true and brave and meek,
  He does not know that he is great;
He looks to heaven with wondering gaze,
  And earth with awe by him is trod;
We marvel at the words he says,
  He, at the silences of God.

Thus on their several ways they go,
   And neither other comprehends,
Yet it was God that made them so,
   And they do serve His several ends;
That seeks for light to walk in it,
   And this for God to live in Him;
One questions with a searching wit,
   The other trusts where all is dim.

Why quarrel with their several parts,
   Where each is good if one is best?
And who shall say that this departs,
   Restful, unto Eternal rest,
While he who loves the light goes down
   Into the darkness of the night?—
Life grows unto its perfect crown,
   And light unto a larger light.

I often spoke to Hilda of the poetry that lay
   In all the rich and wondrous life that compassed us about,
At the firesides of the people, in the wild-flowers by the way,
   In our trials, and our sorrows, in our Faith too, and our doubt.

But she did not care for verses; thought all poets
    must be poor;
  And would rather some more money than be
    sung about in rhyme:
Yet she kissed my cheek and forehead, and vowed
    that she was sure
  I should write a name immortal 'mong the great
    ones of the time.

O she knew that she was stupid; how I ever
    came to wed
  Such a silly girl as she was, she never could
    make out;
But she could not keep the garden, if I would
    have every bed
  Free for birds and beasts and creatures to write
    poetry about.

It was nice to hear the throstles answering on the
    evening breeze,
  And to watch the short, sharp rushes of the
    blackbird on the lawn;
But there would not be a cherry left upon the
    loaded trees,
  And the pease were black with cawing rooks
    about the early dawn.

A shadow fell on me at this; for love, young love, had thrown
  A glamour all about her, wreathed a glory round her face,
Sought in her high inspiration; and one does not like to own
  That his dream is somewhat faded, and a little common-place.

Vexed, and slightly disappointed!—still our love was fond and true,
  And trustful and sufficing; so it did not matter much;
But I sat the more alone, and hid my labour from her view,
  For I felt the poet's shrinking from unsympathetic touch.

And my speech grew shallow to her, and my feeling oft was spent
  In small enforcèd humour to laugh poetry away;
And crackling jests would flicker round the higher sentiment,
  Turning pathos into laughter, and earnest into play.

Of course, it was not good for me; but I could shelter her,
  Belying my own nature; and I scrupled not at that,
If I might but dream in secret when the owlets were astir,
  And hooted from the ivy to the moon-bewildered bat.

And just on this point only there was silence 'twixt us twain;
  But silence bringeth sorrow where the trust should be complete;
Love likes not shallow mirth, too; and a fear sprang up amain,
  That in the deeper life of life we yet might fail to meet.

Not that spinning rhymes and verses is the deeper life of life,
  Though it may be a true fashion which that deeper life shall wear;
But if heart must mate with heart to make the husband and the wife,
  Mind should also match with mind to make the perfect wedded pair.

Not so with me and Hilda; there was love, and
    nothing more :
  But some ballads I had written, brought me
    praise and also pay;
Then she changed her mind about them, as she
    tinkled o'er and o'er
  The little store of guineas that had dropt upon
    her way.

Surely welcome were the guineas; but I had not
    writ for gold,
  And the gold was all she cared for, and I could
    have cursed the thing;
But she had the care of housekeeping, and troubles
    manifold,
  That were bound upon her spirit by the slender
    marriage ring.

I should have thought of that, for it was burden-
    ing her youth—
  Her youth that never knew a care until she
    came to me ;
But I only saw that everything went orderly and
    smooth,
  And wist not of the frets and fears of small
    economy.

Then, the handling of those guineas seemed to
    turn her little head;
  She was sure that I could write a score of
    better songs a week,
And she need not vex her heart about the milk-
    books, or the bread,
  Or the men that came with nasty bills, and
    always looked so sleek.

And she wanted something pretty—a bit of orna-
    ment,
  A dress, or some fresh furnishing to brighten up a
    room ;
And we named them quaintly after, each, its poem,
    as we spent
  The little roll of gold that made her life to bud
    and bloom.

"Noche Triste," was a ballad of the fall of
    Mexico,
  And also a chintz curtain in our little parlour
    hung ;
And a band of scarlet ribbon, knotting up into a
    bow,
  Had its name of "English Harold" from a
    song that I had sung.

Trifles ! yet they lit our home with lamps of sweet
    significance,
  Made every chamber live, and put a soul in
    chairs and stools,
That linked them with our highest, as the moon-
    beams where they glance
  Silver with heavenly beauty even the common
    water-pools.

Trifles ! little homely trifles ; fireside jests that lose
    their way
  Out of doors ; yet what a pathos in their memory
    may dwell !
For I thought my very heart would break when
    coming yesterday
  On that rag of scarlet ribbon fastening up the
    jargonelle.

Twice-paid I deemed my verses when the trifle
    they had brought
  Brightened her evening muslin then, and made her
    face to shine ;
And now it all came back to point the misery of
    our lot,
  As with a twice-told sorrow, in that ribbon's fate
    and mine.

Hilda scarcely read my verses, never sang a song
   of mine,
  Though her voice was like a plaintive bird's, and
     thrilled you through and through;
I have wept to hear her evening hymn, or Psalm
   with crabbèd line,
  Ring through the open casement as the stars
     lit up the blue.

But she scarcely read my verses; even some that
   I had writ
  Of our wooing and our wedding, gave her but
     a passing thought;
I was pleased to see her pleased, but still there
   was a sting in it,
  When she prized my labour only for the thing
     that it had bought.

Yet I would not be disheartened; my purpose only
   rose
  The higher, and my fancies were but cherished
     more and more;
I would seek out fresher fountains whose living
   water flows,
  Unnoticed, in a land where song had rarely
     been before.

I would sing the life I saw—the world that lay
    about our door;
  Its passion and its longing, its error and its
    sin :
It was fresh, if rather sunless, and it deepened
    more and more
  As I tilled the field whose harvest I was fain to
    gather in.

Thus, long and late I brooded, well resolved
    to make my mark
  On the great age we live in, and my silence
    deeper grew;
I went musing in the day-time, and sat mooning
    in the dark,
  And the rush of sudden fancies made my slum-
    bers broken too.

For the vision grew upon me, the more I did
    attain,
  Dwarfing still my poor achievement with some
    glimpse of nobler fruit;
I scarce had caught a measure when some diviner
    strain,
  A-singing sweetly in my heart, would sing the
    other mute.

Those were days of rich invention, like fresh gold-
   fields, when they find
  Nuggets studding the first spadeful, grains that
     yellow all the sand;
One has by and by to crush the quartz — to
   grind the barren mind,
  And pick a little precious thought with weary
     heart and hand.

But those were fruitful times, when thought ran
   faster than the pen,
  And moulds of quaint invention shaped a hundred
     dainty strains,
As I touched with playful fancy the odd
   characters of men
  With kindly humours in their hearts, or maggots
     in their brains.

If I have won a little niche—I know it is but
   small—
  In Fame's proud temple, it was then I won it,
     being true,
And sparing not myself, and without effort natural,
  And singing ever from my heart, and only what
     I knew.

For mine eye was opened wide to all the glory
 and the beauty,
 And also to the error, and the failure, and the
 strife;
My heart had tasted sorrow, as it clung to love
 and duty,
 And I felt my art was deepened with the deep-
 ening of my life.

I sought about among the common facts of com-
 mon day,—
 What chanced me in a corner, or what met me
 in a crowd,—
For the undertones of pathos murmuring softly by
 the way,
 Or quaint, droll humours, mirthful with a laughter
 never loud.

I cared not for the converse of Respectability,
 Choosing rather the blank Innocent that saun-
 tered down the street,
Singing the broken fragment of some weird old
 melody,
 As he drifted, to and fro, with vagrant thought
 and aimless feet.

All the smug and well-conditioned, growing rich
    and growing stout,
  And the men that fussed and wrangled about
    the Kirk and State,
And genteel, superior people, dressing well and
    dining out,
  I found them very dull, though their content was
    very great.

I stored up thoughts and pictures; for I knew that
    Art is long,
  That you cannot rear a temple like a hut of
    sticks and turf;
But I did not think what perils on a woman's life
    may throng,
  Sitting lonely with her thoughts that chafe and
    murmur like the surf.

Ever more and more absorbed, I hardly noted as
    they came
  The changing moods, the chills, the frets that
    daily did increase;
I would dig the deep foundations of a long-abiding
    Fame,
  And wist not that they undermined my home of
    love and peace.

Ah me! that hungry passion! and it looked so
    innocent!
  A minister of love, belike, to brighten all our
    day,
To gild the petty care of life, and homely inci-
    dent,
  As we sat like summer birds, and sang our
    troubles all away!

And yet it was self-seeking, let me paint it as I
    will,
  But the poet's eager craving for the vanity of
    Fame,
But the witchery of Art enchanted with its own
    sweet skill,
  Seeking less to better life, than just to make
    itself a name.

And perchance she saw its shallowness, as I did
    by and by,
  And was truer to the fact, in all her seeming
    common-place,
And the simple, homely method of her quiet life,
    than I
  With my thoughts away in dreamland, and its
    haze about my face.

For I have not won the glory which I lost my
    peace to gain;
  The critic world has praised me in a kindly sort
    of way,
But I have not struck a chord that thrilled the
    common heart of men,
  Nor blazed forth as a star upon the forefront of
    the day.

And yet the passion hankers in me, not to be
    gainsaid.
  In spite of all misgiving, and the verdict of the
    crowd,
And I do not care for poverty, neglect, or little
    bread,
  If I may but spin my verses, though I only spin
    my shroud.

  *   *   *   *   *   *   *   *

That was the first night-frost that blanched our
    young life's tender bloom :
  Not much; and we had love enough to throw
    it off, had I
But taken thought of the pale face that in the
    silent room
  Turned ever to the Kirkyard with a tear-dimmed,
    weary eye :

Turned ever to the Kirkyard where the little grave
    was green
  That buried her young hope, and made her
    motherhood a wail,
Silent and yet unceasing, for the bliss that might
    have been,
  But now was lying in a shroud, and nailed with
    coffin-nail.

I did take thought a little then; and brought an old
    school friend
  To cheer her in her sorrow—but the girl was hard
    as steel,
Who tried, I fear, to mar the peace I hoped that
    she would mend,
  And blended coldest sceptic thought with strangely
    burning zeal :

A girl so unlike Hilda that I wot not how they
    drew
  Together for a moment—sharp-witted, and without
An atmosphere around her mind; but many things
    she knew,
  And had not any light of faith, nor any shade
    of doubt.

Of course we did not know it; but it was unlucky fate
  That brought into my life then such a thread of unbelief,
Confirming troubled fancies that had come to me of late,
  And brooded o'er my life with dim foreboding of new grief.

For pondering, as I could, the things around me, I began
  To piece them, bit by bit, into some pattern of clear thought;
And lo! they grew too vast to fit into my little plan,
  And squared not with the hard and narrow faith that 1 had got.

I had worn my baby-creed, just, as a thing of course, till now,
  Unthinking if it fitted on the grown man as the child;
My mother made it for me when the yet un-shadowed brow
  Was crowned with sunny curls, and the young soul was undefiled.

But it was a thing apart from me, and compassed
    round with dread;
  Unquestioned and unsearched, it lay bathed in
      an awful light,
Sacred as writ which had been sealed by the
    beloved dead,
  And beautiful with memories of piety and right.

But now my mind was darkened o'er with dim, dis-
    turbing doubt,
  And many roots of faith appeared to strike no
      further down
Than customary thoughts that I had never reasoned
    out,
  Nor felt their pressure on my soul to own them,
      or disown.

Could any juggling art transfer the sin that I had
    done,
  Unto another soul, and give his innocence to
      me?
Could any claim of other's right be mine to stand
    upon,
  And urge His sinless sorrow as my justifying
      plea?

And could I think the world lay all beneath the
    wrath of God,
  Seeing it folded in His light, and kept with tender
    care?
Or that the Father's love could grasp an everlast-
    ing rod,
  Nor falter as it hearkened to the wail of dim
    despair?

Could every heart be wholly wicked, every soul
    untrue,
  As if it were a spark from hell that kindled all
    desire?
Could all be set to rights again when God had
    gleaned a few,
  While the harvest of the nations was faggoted
    for fire?

At first I feared the venturous thought, and laid
    it quick aside;
  But still it would return, although in other form
    it came.—
Is He not ever merciful who loved us all, and
    died,
  Gracious to-day and yesterday, and evermore
    the same?

Trembling, I fluttered to and fro, like moth about
  the flame,
  Now saying, "It is light, and I must come unto
    the light:"
Then pausing, for the moth unto a swift destruc-
  tion came,
  When, curious for the light, it left the dim and
    dusky night.

I think it did not grow to be strong-hearted faith
  in me;
  I only dared to doubt, and then made pictures
    of my doubt;
This way the better reason drew that I might
  clearly see;
  That way old custom dragged, and bade me
    cast the reason out.

So wave on wave arose, and burst, and eddied
  back again,
  But still the tide swelled higher till it covered all
    the beach;
I saw old landmarks vanish, yet that smote me not
  with pain,
  Nor leaped my heart with gladness at the truth
    it hoped to reach.

I longed for light; but all the light I found was second-hand;
  Reflected thought that had been tossed about, for ages past,
From surface-minds that vainly claimed alone to understand
  The mystery of the Light that is like shadow on us cast.

They say that doubt is weak; but yet, if life be in the doubt,
  The living doubt is more than Faith that life did never know;
Pulp and jelly of the shell-fish, clasped in bony mail without,
  Crack the joinings and the sutures that the life within may grow.

Could I have just believed with all my heart and soul and mind!
  But faith was slowly breaking up, and parting like a cloud,
And yet the light that through the rifts was glancing from behind,
  Looked sickly in the wavering mist that wrapped it like a shroud.

A zone of large indifference, then, I made, where
 easy hope
 Linked faith and unfaith, arm in arm, and sung
  along the road;
All would somehow yet come right—at least, I did
 not mean to mope,
 If I could not feel the lightness, yet I would
  not feel the load.

God was larger than the creeds: they were the
 cunning compromise
 For unanimous decision of the many and the
  few;
Rafts that leaked at every log, so loose the binding
 of their ties:
 But they floated, and the thoughtless held that
  therefore they were true.

This was the one decree, that God should yet be
 all in all,
 And in the Christ would reconcile all things in
  earth and heaven,
And a new Paradise arise more glorious from the
 Fall,
 And bread of life be sweeter, raised from sin's
  disturbing leaven.

By and by, I hinted lightly at this dawning hope
    of mine
  To Hilda, in a quaint conceit of ballad rudely
    rhymed:
It put her friend in raptures, and she vowed it
    most divine,
  But it seemed a sorry jest to her, and wicked
    and ill-timed.

Well; it was a foolish trifle, burnt well-nigh as soon
    as writ,
  A dream of death, and how all life shall come to
    fulness then,
And how the love that sweetens earth, and mirth
    that brightens it
  Could never darken Heaven, for God had given
    them unto men.

Was it strange, when Hilda frowned, that I should
    turn me to her friend,
  Who clapped her hands, ecstatic, and would
    have me read again?
Perhaps she overdid it; and it turned out in the
    end
  That she was false and faithless—but I did not
    know her then.

Maybe, I should have seen that there was nothing in my rhyme
  To lift up eyes of worship, softly swimming in a tear,
Or to part the eager lips with breathless rapture, all the time,
  As the humour of the dreamer dropt upon the listening ear.

No doubt, she overdid it, turning up her thin, brown face
  With the dark eyes and eager; I had called her Caberfae,
She looked so like a startled deer that, in a lonely place,
  Lifts her head among the bracken at the dawning of the day.

And somehow, after that, she filled my life up, as the tide
  Creeps, beneath the waving tangles, up the sloping, shingly shore,
And along the quiet sands, and softly lapping at your side,
  Girds about you ere you wot, and is behind you and before.

She would look through books of reference, and
    mark the places right,
  And copy papers nicely, and be useful fifty
    ways;
And sometimes on the darkling thought would
    glance a piercing light,
  Or with woman's nice suggestion touch a senti-
    ment or phrase.

I looked to her for sympathy, I leant on her for
    aid;
  Fanatical for Reason, still she loved the poet's
    Art,
Or vowed she loved it dearly; and how cleverly
    she played,
  With artillery of praise upon the outworks of the
    heart!

Ere long, I did not care to hear her raptures,
    for they came
  To be mere ejaculations, monotonous, without
Any critical discernment; and I felt a growing
    shame
  At the lauds which she kept singing, and the things
    they were about.

And, besides, my floating doubts, which were like
    mists that slowly trail
  O'er the mountains, adding mystery and grandeur
    to their shapes,
Were in her a chilling drizzle, or a driving sleet
    and hail,
  Hiding sun and moon and stars, and all the
    shining seas and capes.

I could not cast her off, but yet I heeded not how
    soon
  She took herself away now, with that bitter sneer
    of hers;
She was as coldly chaste as are "the glimpses of
    the moon,"
  But she laughed at all the faiths of men, and
    all their characters.

And I saw that Hilda pined away—she did not
    fret nor frown,
  But, whatever our discourse, she let a pallid
    silence linger
On her lips, from hour to hour, while moving
    slowly up and down,
  From the knuckle to the point, the marriage-ring
    upon her finger.

For Hilda had a faith serene, clear as the evening star,
  Keen-piercing through the changeful glow with its unchanging gleam,
Wheeling in some calm zone where neither doubts nor tremours are,
  Nor shadowy, dim misgivings, that perchance we only dream.

And now she was amazed because old Faiths broke up in me,
  With little feeling of a loss, or hope of higher gain,
But like the ice-pack piled and crashing on the fog-banked sea,
  The which her love beheld with fear and shivering and pain.

BOOK SECOND.

Hilda, Saint-Wife.

HILDA'S DIARY.

March, 18—

WINIFRED Urquhart and I, when we were tall
 school-girls,
Chatting of wooings and weddings while twisting
 our hair up in curls,
Or whispering some hush-secret, which was not
 secret a bit,
Only we were confidential, and made a secret of it—
Winnie and I made a paction, silly things that we
 were!
That she would be sure to tell me, and I must
 be sure to tell her,
Whoever, first of us, wedded, all the bitter and sweet
Of the life of marriage that makes the life of a
 woman complete;

The hope, the fear, and the bliss too, we were to set down all,
And none of our Gardens of Eden be hid by a hedge or a wall.

So now she writes me a letter, all underlined, to say
She trusts that I do not forget the promise I made that day;
Hints that, perhaps, I might keep a Diary locked with a key,
And sacred To Early Friendship, which no other eye should see;
And hopes that I will not act like commonplace wives, who drop
Their friends and their French and pianos, and put to the Past a full stop,
So to begin a new paragraph all about beeves and muttons,
Darning, and troubles with servants, and gentlemen's shirts and buttons.
Why does marriage, she adds, so often a woman degrade?
Why is the wife so silly, who was ever so bright as a maid?
Why should a husband like to fallow her intellect,

And starve it on housekeeping cares that lower her
    self-respect?
But she is sure that mine is all that he ought to be,
Worthy of love and devotion, almost worthy of me.
Yet, O the young love of girls! it is purer, truer,
    and better!
And so she concludes with a prayer for a long and
    an early letter.

This has set me a-thinking that, maybe, I ought
    to write
The things that my heart is full of, as the noon
    of heaven with light,
The thoughts that I had not before, which give me
    a larger life,
And the bliss that never I knew till he called me
    his own little wife.
Not that I mean to keep a silly promise like that—
Winnie is clever and scheming; I know what she
    wants to be at.
Give her a word, good or bad, and she'd spin such
    a web from the hint,
And colour a meaningless phrase with so suspicious
    a tint,
That folk would begin to whisper, sure there was
    something amiss:

And then she would write me, bewailing the world
   and its wickedness.
Dearly she loves a mystery, dearly she loves to be
   thought
To know what she ought not to know, and to wit
   what none else ever wot :
For Winnie is clever and scheming, even when she
   looks like a fool ;
She was not liked by the girls, and she was not
   happy at school,
But I came to be fond of her, rather, by having to
   take her part,
When others were hard upon her, and said that
   she had not a heart ;
Which is not true, I am sure, nor yet the tales that
   they told
Of wicked books she had read before she was
   twelve years old.
I have heard that, since she came home, she culti-
   vates science, and writes,
And lectures over the country, most of the winter
   nights,
Having her hair cut short, and her finger-tips black
   with ink :—
But Winnie could never forget what is due to a lady,
   I think.

I am going to write in my book, but not for her
    eyes to see:
Ought I to hide it from him who keeps not a thought
    from me?
O there is something in marriage, like the veil of
    the temple of old,
That screened the Holy of Holies with blue and
    purple and gold;
Something that makes a chamber where none but
    the one may come,
A sacredness too, and a silence, where joy that is
    deepest is dumb.
And it is in that secret chamber where chiefly my
    days are passed,
With a sense of something holy, and a shadow of
    something vast,
Till he comes, who alone is free to come and to
    go as he will,
Till he comes, and the brooding silence begins to
    pulse and thrill.
O come, for my heart is weary, waiting, my love,
    for thee!
I will lock my bliss from the world, but my love
    shall have ever the key.

March, 18—

When I remember the way we girls were wont to talk
Up in our rooms at night, or out on the daily walk,
It seems like an unreal echo, ever so far away
From the clear realm of nature, and light of the sun and the day.
Yet it sounded to us, at the time, like absolute reason and good,
As we chattered of woman's rights, and babbled in wrathful mood
Of Maries, thoughtful and wise, that often were met at school,
Changed into careful Marthas under a husband's rule,
Heedless of mental culture, losing their nimble wits,
To be housemaids dusting the rooms, or cookmaids turning the spits.
Winnie was great on that—I thought she was eloquent even,
As the small face kindled up with a light, as it were, from heaven,
Vowing the wife became a traitor to woman in this,
Betraying a noble cause for a petting word or a kiss;
Wronging her husband, too, by giving a lower aim
Of self-indulgence to life, which he knew not at home till she came.

What greater wrong could she do him than teach him only to care
For dainties, and kickshaws, and slippers, and naps in the easy chair?—
But Nature is more than Logic, and wedlock is more than we
Dreamed of then in our folly; and great is the change now in me:
Motherhood, if it should come, will work more wonders still,
For love it is all in all, and it does whatsoever it will;
Dusting, darning, drudging, nothing is great or small,
Nothing is mean or irksome, love will hallow it all;
Sacrifice there is none if only I see him glad,
And all my pleasure is gone if he be heavy and sad.

April, 18—

Past is the honeymoon; and I think it was not so good
As the home-coming together, with quiet, thoughtful mood.
Then our life truly began: it was like a dream before—
A dream in a boat while the pale moon glimmered from sea to shore,

And we went swaying about still under the stars, and heard
Dreamily plashing billow, and dreamily whispered word.
Why should we go a-jaunting when the heart wants to repose
From agitation of bliss, and to know whereto it grows?
Nothing felt real to me then, or brought me the feeling of rest,
As we sped hither and thither, like birds flying far from the nest,
Hid in the bosk of the greenwood, where they are longing to be,
And cosy and warm, and sweet with the scent of the sheltering tree.
I did not like then to say it, because all his plans had been laid
To visit some beautiful spot which poets had famous made,
Or look on some ancient Abbey that sweetly went down to decay,
Wrapt in the ivy green, amid trees in the lichen grey,
And all with me there beside him, he said, to brighten the view,

And bathe it for him in a light which for ever would
 make it new.
Therefore my voice was silent; but O, how I wearied
 to see
The house-fire which love was to kindle, the home
 where my life was to be!
For all the pert maids at the inns where we hoped
 for a little to hide,
Scanning my bonnets and dresses, would smirk at
 the new-made bride;
Scarcely a railway porter but knew my trunks to
 be out
Fresh on a marriage trip, and led me, blushing,
 about,
While Claud was looking so handsome and self-
 possessed, like a king,
Proud and tender and ready, and seeing to every-
 thing.
It is not nice to be stared at by everyone that
 you meet,
As they smile and whisper together, and scan you
 from head to feet.
I knew not the rest of love till we sat in our
 little white room,
Close together, and watched the stars coming out of
 the gloom,

In the hush of a raptured moment, his strong arm
    clasping me round,
As on his bosom I leant to feel all the peace
    I had found;
And he said, "We will fold our wings now, for here
    I have made you a nest,
And lined it warm with the down of the love that
    warms my breast."
O, he can say such things! And I cannot say
    them to him;
I am quietest when I am gladdest; but my heart
    was filled to the brim.
Just a moment before, and my trembling would not
    cease,
But now the shiver was stilled in a thrill of bliss
    and peace.

April, 18—

Our home is a bright little cottage, half-smothered
    in yellow rose,
Not yet blooming, however; a still river sullenly
    flows
Deep at the foot of a broomy brae, and the leaping
    trout

Ripple its gloom in the evening as May-flies flicker
    about.
Nor is it all so sullen, for down in a farther reach
It leaps and sparkles and gleams o'er the stones of
    a pebbly beach,
Under the birch and the hazel, just coming to leaf,
    and there are
Blue-bell patches of sky made bright with the primrose star.
Behind is a group of great fir-trees, five of them,
    red-armed firs,—
Druid sisters he calls them,—that moan when the
    night-wind stirs;
Last of a great pine forest that stubs the heath
    with its roots
For miles, till you come to a tarn where gulls and
    little round coots
Are dipping and diving all day in a quiet solitude;
There the bee haunts, and the air is blithe, and
    the lapwings brood.
I hear the curlew scream, and the grouse-cock
    crowing at dawn,
And yet when I stand at the door, where the cowslips laugh on the lawn—
It is only a patch of green turf, enough to pasture
    a lark—

I see the sleepy old town, and the spires of the
    Minster dark,
And catch a glimpse of the sea-waves white on the
    yellow sand,
Where the river leaps at the bar, and the coastguard
    houses stand.
We have a bright little garden down on a sunny slope,
Bordered with sea-pinks, and sweet with the songs
    and the blossoms of hope.
O it is all too good for me; often I catch myself
    singing
In very lightness of heart, and I seem like the birds
    to be winging
Merry from room to room, as they flutter from bush
    to tree,
And each has her mate a-coming, and mine, too, is
    coming to me.

Am I wrong to be always so happy? This world
    is full of grief;
Yet there is laughter of sunshine, to see the crisp
    green on the leaf,
Daylight is ringing with song-birds, and brooklets are
    crooning by night;
And why should I make a shadow where God
    makes all so bright?

Earth may be wicked and weary, yet cannot I help
   being glad;
There is sunshine without and within me, and how
   should I mope or be sad?
God would not flood me with blessings, meaning
   me only to pine
Amid all the bounties and beauties He pours upon
   me and mine;
Therefore will I be grateful, and therefore will I
   rejoice;
My heart is singing within me; sing on, O heart
   and voice.

May, 18—

Winnie has writ me again—she offers a visit in June;
Some day she must come, I daresay; but that is
   an age too soon.
What could I do with her? I should be like one
   reading a book,
Lost in the story and passion, while she would
   be eager to look
Over my shoulder to find out what was absorbing
   me so,
And why, when my heart is so happy, the tears
   are so ready to flow;

And now she would hurry, and now would tarry my turning the leaf;
And I'd hate her in less than a week; and I know it would end in grief.
Alone! I must be alone, to read my romance, for the plot
Is only slowly unfolding; and O what a hero I've got!
Noble and true and brave, all that a hero should be;
So much better than I am; and great is his love to me;
Yet not greater than mine is, save that his mind is more,
For O I love him, I love, as a God I could almost adore.
That makes me tremble at times, for O if an idol I make,
What if my idol were broken? Truly my heart it would break.
What, if heaven should be wroth at my shrining and sainting a man
Sinful and mortal as I? Yet God too I love, all I can;
My heart is truer to Him the more I am loved and caressed;
And surely He cannot be jealous of love He has bidden and blessed.

June, 18—

We have walks as the evenings lengthen; sometimes over the moor,
Many-tinted and shadowed; brisk is the air there and pure
Among the brown heath and the bracken that now from its snake-like bonds,
Under the sun's deft fingers, is slowly uncoiling its fronds;
Close-packed now, by-and-by they, overlapping, will hide
The flower of the slender orchis purpling close by their side.
Dry on the knolls is the whin-bush, massing its golden bloom;
The cotton-grass low in the marshes tosses its small white plume;
And from the hollows is wafted the scent of bog-myrtle or birch
Fragrant after the rain; but, best of all, is the search
Among the roots of the heather for stag-moss' antlers green
Branching over the earth, far-spreading, and rarely seen.

Here and there is a cottage, too, looking just like the heath,
Green on the roof with house-leek, brown with its turf-wall beneath.
Children play at the door, they are dirty and happy and fair,
Sunbrowned all of their faces, sunbleached their lint-white hair;
The mother is milking the cow, the dog lies coiled in the sun,
The fowls for the roost are making, and the labourer's day is done.
Sometimes we rest on a bank, and hear in the evening calm,
Just as the stars come out, the *sough* of their grateful psalm.

Often we go to the sea-marge, where the long sands give place
To a belt of dark red storm-beaten crags, which grimly face
The baffled billows that lie ever panting below at their feet,
Or gurgling in black-throated caves where still they mine and beat.

Perched on the cliff is a village, and far in the cove below
The boats are beached on the shingle, waiting the tide to flow;
Hard-visaged, bunchy women are baiting the lines in hope,
Or carrying laden creels, slow, up the long, shelving slope,
Or spreading their fish on the rocks, or welcoming men from the sea,
As the lugger trips daintily in, and the flapping sail is free.

One thing strikes me about my husband's way with the folk,
Whether the moorland shepherds, or fishermen perched on the rock.
Freely we enter their homes, for he seems to be known to them all,
And knows who is there in the corner, and who in the bed in the wall,
And the idiot dreamily singing by the grandam racked with pain,
And the lad that went off to the sea, and has never come back again—

All the home life of the people, their good and
    their evil hap,
So every door flies open just after a warning tap,
And everywhere he is met with a welcome glad and
    free;
The dogs come fawning upon him, the children get
    up on his knee,
Great, rough hands are held out to give him a hearty
    grip,
And the mother's face is shining as he kisses the
    baby's lip.
Of course they are happy to see me, too, for my
    husband's sake,
Only they daintily touch me, as fearful perchance
    I may break,
And, making ungainly curtseys, they have not a
    word to say;
But O I am proud to see him so loved in this
    lovingest way.

Sometimes I think, for myself, I would like to tidy
    the room,
To open the window a bit, and get rid of the
    smoke and the gloom,
To teach the children a lesson, or read a page
    from the Book

To the sick man tossed on his pillow, or the old
　　man propped in his nook.
But he does not try, in the least, to do any good,
　　and yet
Somehow they seem to like him all the better for it.
He is just like one of themselves, and talks of the
　　weather and crops,
The ewes and gimmers and lambs, or the luggers and
　　nets and ropes,
The take of fish, or the beds of mussels they have
　　for bait,
Or the old man's aching bones, or the teething
　　baby's state,
Laughing and joking with all, or telling a story,
　　perhaps,
To the children gaping around him, while grandfather
　　nods and naps;
Yet somehow, all the time, he seems as if reading a
　　book
Full of nature and humour, and leaves with a
　　thoughtful look.

Once I hinted that I would gladly be doing some
　　good
Among these neighbours of ours: and he said in his
　　gentlest mood,

"Yes, I suppose it is right to do all the good that
   you can;
Only don't break up the peace of their homes, with a
   cut-and-dry plan
Of tracts and visits and lessons, and scolding the
   women for dirt,
And tramping on everyone's toes, and sitting on
   everyone's skirt.
For when you know them as I do, and all their
   sorrows and cares,
The brave hearts they keep through it all, their
   patience, their faith, and the prayers,
Self-forgetting, that thrill here loud on the stormy
   shore
For those on the stormy sea, they never may look
   on more,
Then you may feel like me, half-ashamed of the
   good you can do,
Compared with the good you are getting from
   lives so human and true.
But try it—you're better than I—only mind they
   have hearts like your own;
And hearts philanthropic, at times, have the trick
   of the old hearts of stone.

November, 18—

What is it ails me now? I hardly have written a line
For days and weeks and months in this private record of mine.
I seemed to have nothing to say, and I did not seem to care,
And the days have gone wearily by, though there was not a cloud in the air.
I think that my love is more, yet life is little and low,
And surely a fulness of life from a fulness of love should grow,
For love is summer, when all should be a-blooming and singing;
Yet none of the old things now the old sweet bliss are bringing.
I go a-dreaming and weary, every day and all;
Something is aching within me, I fret at the simplest call
Of common-place duty that once I went about cheerful and gay,
Tripping and singing, light-hearted, all through the hours of the day.

Everything burdens me now; and I could cry at a kiss
From the dear lips that I love so : What is the meaning of this?
I am not unhappy; at least, I have nothing to make me : and yet
My gladness is broken and dashed, and comes by the mood and the fit :
I weep when I'm left alone; and when he comes home, there are tears
That mix with the smile of my greeting, and fill him with fond, loving fears.
I want to be cheerful and happy, I want to be busy and good,
Yet I lounge through the day, doing nothing, and plain like the dove in the wood.
What can it be? And my ring, too, will slip to my finger tip,
And it gives me a catch in the throat, and a pain, and a quivering lip :
I know it is silly, and yet I cannot get rid of the fear
That his love may grow loose as my ring, and be lost while I think it is here.

November, 18—

I wonder if every student sits brooding far into the night,
And hides from the wife of his bosom the thing he is fain to write.
Can it be right to conceal the work he is labouring at?
I want to sit up beside him, but he will not listen to that;
Yet rest I cannot; I lie there, sleepless, and feigning to sleep,
When, in the hush of the darkness, soft to my side he will creep,
Fearing to rouse me lying, broad-awake, all through the hours,
Watching the moonbeams flitting, or hearing the patter of showers,
The grey owl screech to the bat, or the moan of the throbbing sea,
Or puzzling over the house-books, which will not come right with me.—
We are not rich, and, maybe, I do not keep house as I might,
Though I want to be thrifty, and debt is a thing that I hate outright;

Still there is waste, no doubt, and he has a right to complain,
And maids are so careless, and break things that cannot be mended again;
And will have their young men coming: and how can I say them nay,
When I recall how I longed to see him at evening grey?
I scrimp and save, and, at times, I am almost weary of life;
It would have been better for him had he married a managing wife.
Yet all my cares were as nothing if only my husband were right,
If he were not so silent by day, if he were not so dreamy at night,
Cared for things in the house as he cared for them once on a time,
Sat by my side in the evenings, and made my life sweet and sublime,
Did he not joke at my questions—a wife is not meant for sport,
Always put off with a jest; and jesting is not his forte.
Yet O he loves me, he loves; and I hate myself when I complain,
Only the hunger of love ever breeds dream-visions of pain.

What is he always writing? Sometimes I tremble
    to think,
What, if it be of Religion? what, if he be on the brink
Of falling away from the Faith, and the way which
    his fathers trod,
And, as the minister told us, out of the hand of
    God?
Rarely he goes to Church, though he tells me I
    ought to go,
When the kirk-bells on the Sabbath are chiming
    soft and low;
"You have your window," he says, "for outlook
    on all the vast,
Dim, everlasting hills, and the shadows on earth
    they cast,—
The old church-window that shines with white-winged
    angel forms,
And martyred saints they are bearing from earth's
    most bitter storms;
And life would be dark to you, dear, lacking the
    light that it brings,
Even though the cobwebs dim the aureoles now, and
    the wings.
I have my outlook too, but not so pretty as yours
With dreams of the saintly souls, and the love that
    all endures;

Colder my light and harder, but clearer, at least,
   to me,
For cobwebbed angels somehow help not my vision
   to see.
But to the same Eternal, we look for the breaking
   day,
Of an age that is surely coming, when shadows
   shall flee away."
I am troubled at sayings like these, though I
   hardly know what they mean,
And I pray that he yet may see the truth which my
   heart has seen.
For O he loves me, loves me, ever so tender and
   true!—
And yet if he loves not God, O what shall my
   poor heart do?

December, 18—

Last night we went to Thorshaven; the things that
   I heard and saw
Of the "work" now going on there have filled me
   with wonder and awe.
I had been told of their meetings, and how they
   rarely would cease

Till many were conscience-stricken, and many were
   filled with peace;
How the whole village was changed—its drunkards
   sober and calm,
Lips that were wont to blaspheme now thrilling the
   air with a psalm;
Boats were launched with a prayer, and the oars
   were timed to a hymn;
And when the lines were set, or the ropes and
   the sails were trim,
Some one took up the tale of the fishers on Galilee,
And told how the Lord drew nigh to them walking
   over the sea.
These were the marvels I heard, and O my heart
   longed to be there
Where the good Spirit was working, and grace was
   like dew in the air
Dropping on thirsty grass, and making it live
   anew.
Maybe my husband, beholding, would see that the
   Gospel was true;
Maybe his soul would be touched; and maybe my
   own dull faith
Would be refreshed and revived, for it seemed at
   the point of death.

The night was starry and cold, but just a night for
a walk,
Brisk, in the tingling air; and at first I was fain to
talk,
His coming had made me so glad then, only my
thoughts would not rest,
Flitting about like the swallows that twitter around
their nest,
And then skim away to the river, and dip where
the shadows lie
Clear in the glassy calm, which they flick with their
wings as they fly;
So would I chatter a little; but by-and-by thought
was away
To the village perched on the cliff, and the people
there gathered to pray,
So that in silence at length, arm in arm, swiftly we
sped
On by the beetling crags, till we came to a low
rude shed
Roofed with the upturned hull of a wreck that had
drifted ashore,
Battered by surf on the shingle there for a month
and more;
Gallantly once she had ridden the waves, and the
tempest braved,

And true hearts then had been lost in her; now in
    her wreck they were saved.
Crowds were thronging about it; there was a crowd
    inside
Singing a hymn that blended well with the wash
    of the tide—
A wail of sorrow for sin, that swelled to a yearning
    hope;
Then I heard some one praying, but caught not
    the words nor the scope,
For many were sobbing aloud; we squeezed a little
    way in,
Under a guttering candle stuck in a sconce of tin,
The flame blown about by the wind, and shedding
    uncertain light
Down on rough weather-beat faces. Clear and cold
    was the night;
Outside, the passionless moon and the quiet stars;
    but here,
O what a tempest of trouble and sorrow, and anguish
    and fear!
O what a peace, at last, that folded its wings on a
    calm
Throng of spirits entranced, and singing a grateful
    psalm!

He was a keen-eyed, wiry, beetled-browed man who spoke,
The pale-faced smith of our village; and simply he pled with the folk,
His voice half saying half singing the faithful message he bore
Weirdly and hoarse, like the waves that were crashing down on the shore.
It was not aught that he said—he was just a plain, blunt man,
Earnest, I thought, and acquainted with God and the wonderful Plan
Saving by surety of Him who hung for our sins on the cross,
And tasted of death for our guilt, that we might gain in His loss—
A plain, blunt man, not a scholar; sometimes his sayings were odd,
Nor could I help a smile though he spake of the great thoughts of God;
But of the fisher-folk no one smiled, let him say what he would;
It was not a season for laughter, nor were they at all in the mood.
"The strength of sin is the law," he said; "it is like the tree

Serpents take for a purchase in lands where the serpents be;
Clean and straight is its trunk, as the law too is right in its scope,
Slippery the coils and the folds round its bark that are twined like a rope,
Crushing each bone of its victim, and grinding the life out, within;
So is the purchase of Law, for breaking the soul by its sin:
O how feeble and helpless we are in its terrible grip!
For the law cannot be broken, and these knots never will slip!
Coming along the street, I saw the old serpent to-night,
Plainly as eyes could behold him—and O 'twas a sorrowful sight!—
Coiling round old men and children, as in a statue I know,
Carved with his cunningest art by a wise Greek ages ago,
But there to save his children the Father was wrestling grim,
Here, with shouting and singing, they were all worshipping him.

Yes, I have seen the old serpent, the Devil, the father of lies;
And he had not a hoof or a horn, or a tail to whisk at the flies;
Old men were buying his curses, children were taking his fire
Home to their mothers in bottles, as briskly as hell could desire.
Busy he is at Thorshaven, sails in your luggers with you,
Never a boat goes to sea but the devil is one of the crew;
You carry him too in your creels, and he is defiling your way,
With swearing and lying and cheating, and breaking the Sabbath day,
And sins that I will not speak of, sins that all of you know.—
But O the blood of the Lamb it will wash you whiter than snow."
Always he came back to that, the blood that was shed for sin,
Cleansing our way on the earth, and purging the soul within;
He shewed to me all my guilt, he shewed me the love of God

Until I wept at the plague of my heart, and the way I had trod,
And the pity that sought me out, and the grace that died for me.
And all were sobbing and swaying about like the waves of the sea.
Then one dropped on the floor, and writhed in a foaming fit;
"Glory to God," cried the preacher, "He'll snaffle the fiend with his bit;
Let her alone; while the devil is wrestling with her we will pray;
Peace will come like the stars, and light as the dawn of the day."
Then another was smitten, and lay there with never a breath
In her thin nostril, it seemed, and pallid and cold as death;
I thought she was gone, till at length a smile of serenest grace
Broke on her lips, and beamed all over her lovely face.
She was the first to find Peace, and she said, "I have seen my love;
He's not in the depths of the ocean, but high in the heavens above;

His head is not twined round with tangles, but
    wreathed with a wreath of palm,
And lo! in his hand is a harp, and loud in his
    mouth is a psalm."
(Her lover was drowned last spring, and his body
    had never been found,
Till she saw him in faith, in her trance, and robed
    in white raiment and crowned.)
Thus it went on for hours, at first with the women,
    but then,
Ere long, the power and the wonder smote the
    strong hearts of the men;
Awed and amazed I stood, unable to stir from
    the place,
Sometimes thinking my heart might be touched by
    its marvellous grace,
Sometimes feeling my flesh creep at an unearthly voice,
Sometimes thrilling to hear their songs who for joy
    did rejoice.
At length there fell a great calm, and the lights
    were glimmering dim,
And the moon was low in the heaven, when we
    sang the parting hymn.

On the way homeward I said, "Surely the Lord was
    there;"

And he, "No doubt, and up in yon star too, and
    everywhere;
Hard to say where He is not. Wonderful? Yes,
    I admit;
Hard to say what is not wonderful, when you look
    closely at it;
Why, I have wondered for hours at a flower, or a
    lichened stone,
Or star-moss red on the heath, or a star-fish dry
    as a bone
On the grey shore, till the tide-wave brought back
    the pulses of life.
But does not yon queer evangelist tell a good story,
    dear wife?
Done them some good, you think? Ah! Well, we
    will hope so at least;
God is a chemist who works with stuff that would
    sicken a priest.
I think it did good to that girl whose lover was
    drowned at sea,
Gave her some comfort she wished; but it would
    not do good to me!"
Thus I come home heavy-hearted; he always is
    ready to mock,
Turning from anything serious, still with a good-
    humoured joke.

December, 18—

Now I know why he sits so late and alone in his room,
And why there comes over his face that shadow I took for gloom,
Which falls like a sudden haze all over the summer sky,
And makes him look stony and cold, with a dream-like fixëd eye,
Seeing not what we see, for the outer vision is dim,
As he looks on a world unseen, and hears it singing to him.
Often it filled me with fear, for I thought he was wroth with me;
But he is not angry at all—only trying, he says, to see
Thoughts that are hard to get at, and hardly worth getting when done;
But the fool's habit of dreaming he learnt when living alone;
I must not fancy he sulks; he was only a bit of a poet,
Dram-drinking verses in secret, and hoping that no one would know it.

So then he brought me some poems, writ for our marriage-day,
"Orange-blossoms" he calls them, "A wreath for a wedding gay."
I do not know that I care for poems—though hymns are sweet—
I do not want to be talked of, or sung some day in the street,
And at the time I was plagued with these horrible tradesmen's books,
And maybe my words were dry, and listless also my looks.
They are nice enough verses, I fancy—but O those dreadful bills!
And he just laughs at my trouble, and calls it the care that kills—
A faithless terror of bakers and butchers and Philistines,
Unworthy a true believer in orthodox, sound divines.

Well, they are pretty verses, and so I will write them here—
But how can he pen such trifles with that shadow of debt so near?

ORANGE-BLOSSOMS.

BUDDING.

It was the gloaming of the day,
   And first pale glimmer of the moon,
The fishing-boats were in the bay,
And to and fro they seemed to sway,
    Rhythmic, to a mystic tune,
    In the pale glimmer of the moon.

We sat us on a thymy bank,
   Where sea-pink and the wild-rose grew,
And blue campanulas were rank,
And wild geranium blossoms drank
    Red sunsets that enriched their hue,
    And pansies twinkled, gold and blue.

And fronting us the broad sea-sand
   Spread, ribbed and freckled, to the spray
Crisp-curving to the curving land,
And plashing on the pebbly strand;
    Beyond, the vague, vast waters lay
    Lazily heaving in the bay.

Three children played along the beach
   With laughter, as the small waves broke;
I heard their laughter and their speech
Rippling along the sandy beach,
   Though fear and trouble in me woke
   Like the waves surging as they broke.

I told my love, and for a space
   She gazed out far away from me.
O throbbing heart, how still the place!
Was that a smile that lit her face?
   Or but the moon drawn from the sea
   To kiss the lips that can bless me?

I told the love you knew before;
   You said, I did not need to tell,
And that you would not answer more,
For that I also knew before
   The secret of your heart so well
   It did not need that you should tell.

BLOOMING.

O bleak November morning chill,
   When trees are bare, and haws are ripe!

Hopping upon my window sill
    I heard the cheery redbreast pipe ;
And through the crackling twigs there ran
A twitter of birds since day began.

With great frost-ferns the panes were white,
    The fields were white with dusty snow,
The trees, all crystalled overnight,
    In white robes made a ghostly show,
And where the fountain used to drip
The ice had clutched it in its grip.

Chanticleer at barn-door crew,
    Geese were gobbling 'mong the stubble,
My dog in circles round me flew,
    Barking loud at its shadow-double,
And ploughed the crisp frost with his nose
Right where the cluttering partridge rose.

Crowding close, the dainty sheep
    Nibbled by the bridled brook,
The hare pricked up her ears to leap
    Behind the ricks to a quiet nook ;
Knee-deep in straw the black ox lowed,
His every breath like a steaming cloud.

SAINT-WIFE.

Jenny, looking tossed and tumbled,
    Stept out with her milking-pails;
Yawning Robin crept and grumbled,
    Blowing on his finger-nails,
Tingling fingers, purple-tipped,
Sharply by the frost-wind nipped.

But I laughed at ice and snow,
    Shouting to the shrill north-wind :
She is mine, I said, and no
    Winter in the world I find;
Love, my life is filled with thee,
And all is summer now with me.

BURSTING.

O pathway through the meadow green,
    And thou, grey style, beneath the thorn,
    And murmurous river softly borne
In dimpling ripplets hardly seen,

Sweet path by happy footsteps worn,
    If all our visions linger there,
    The poet now shall find thine air,
More fancy-full than early morn.

We wandered in a dreamland fair,
  Beside the huge, coiled willow trees,
  Discoursing of a life to please
The Man who took our grief and care.

Not ours the dull, ignoble ease
  Of cushioned seats, or routs and balls,
  Brain-dulling dinners, civil calls,
And poor respectabilities;

Not ours to care for marble halls;
  A modest home, and frugal fare,
  With love for cobwebbed wines and rare,
And peace for pictures on the walls—

For more than these we would not care:
  But generous culture should be ours,
  And pious use of all our powers,
And knowledge, as the primal pair

Knew all the beasts and birds and flowers;
  And with our best we'd serve the Best,
  And in His goodness find our rest,
Untroubled through the years and hours.

April, 18--

These were the first of the poems he read to me
    up in my room;
By and by others came, soon, like the coming of
    spring with its bloom;
And we are rich now and happy, and everything
    goes quite smooth;
All the newspapers praise him, but do not say
    half of the truth:
I keep them all in a book, and read them often
    alone.
They make me angry at times, when they speak
    in a critical tone,
But I am happy and proud, for now I am no-
    body's debtor,
Paying odd things with a verse which he writes me
    as fast as a letter.
He laughs at me, vowing that poets should never
    pay bills, but draw
At large on the shopkeeping world, exempt from
    all action at law;
Honouring bakers and butchers enough by eating
    their things;
For angels pay not a jot for repairing the plumes
    of their wings,

And bees are not charged by the flowers they visit
    for tapping the honey—
I am not quite sure what he means, but I know he
    is loose about money.

May, 18—

Sick! I am sure death is coming: I never have felt
    like this;
Such giddy sinkings and swimmings, and fainting
    away into bliss!
Life in the swooning of life, as if the soul fluttered
    within,
Panting, exhausted, in hope to escape from the
    body of sin!
Heart, O my heart so unquiet, why wilt thou not
    be at rest?
Clinging to this life of trouble, shrinking from life
    of the blest!
Better to be with Jesus! yet husband and home too
    are dear;
And O if my love be a sin, I cannot help sinning,
    I fear.
All other idols are broken, this one I never can
    break.
Could I be shut out of heaven because of the heaven
    that I make

Out of my true love to him, and out of his great
    love to me,
Arching as deep blue sky still over a deep blue sea?

If this be death, as I take it, one thing fain would
    I do,
Ere I go hence to the world where all things are
    made new:
Again with my husband I'd walk, on the quiet Sab-
    bath day,
When bells from the old kirk chiming call Christian
    souls to pray,
Down by the green footpath, and the sweet-briar
    hedge that leads
Straight to the house of the Lord through the
    clover-scented meads;
Under the high-arched roof there meekly to sit by
    his side,
In love to remember the Love that bled for us
    once and died.
O it were good to think, if I should be taken
    from him,
That once we sat there together, where falls the
    light chastened and dim
Through the tall thin-shafted windows on hallowed
    bread and wine,

And vows that we vowed together, of life for the love divine.
I cannot die till we do it: God would not call me hence,
A broken life and unfinished, with a fruitless influence.

June, 18—

Ah me! we plot and plan, but the great God orders all;
And that is not good to Him, which good we are fain to call.
O how I longed and hoped for the high communion day!
O how my heart leaped up when he did not say me nay!
O how I prayed, and was glad and tremulous through the Fast!
O how happy I was, with my hand on his arm, at last,
Gravely pacing together, down by the broomy brae,
Along by the sweet-briar hedge, and the clover-scented way,
All the maids robed in white, and the men in their sober black,

Sweet birds a-singing, and sweet bells ringing; and Paradise back!
Better I never had spoken; better he had not gone!
Better a yearning sorrow than a heart that is turned to stone!

What had come over our Pastor, he so gentle and mild,
Leading his flock to still waters as father leadeth his child,
That day of all days, to preach terrors of wrath and hell,
Darkening God's house with smoke of those in the pit that dwell?
O it was dreadful to listen! The very Psalms that he chose
Rung in the ear like curses hurled at the heads of foes;
The prayers were dry and dewless, and hard; and my heart grew sick,
To glance at my husband's face with its curious laughing trick:
I knew, in that furtive glance, that my hope was worse than lost,
And that, in my effort to save, I had perilled and harmed him most.

Pained there we sat in our pews, the victims of one man's mood,
And vainly tried to be patient; and vainly tried to be good;
E'en the sweet symbols of sorrow and love of the Crucified
Failed to lighten the gloom, for he took not his place by my side.
Never I sat at the Table so barren of grace as then,
Joyless and undevout, and wroth at the thoughts of men.
I had brought to the living water a thirsting soul with care,
And there was no living water, but a broken cistern there.

When we came home he sat alone in his room for a while;
But all that night he was gentle; and said, at last, with a smile;
"You want to know what I think of our minister's work to-day;
But shrink to ask me outright, for the wild words you fear I may say.

Why should you dread me, Hilda? You wished to do me some good;
So did the Parson, no doubt, if he only had understood
The right way of going about it. He made a mistake; that is all;
Hell is the weak point, you see, and a cleverer general
Were fain to conceal the spot where the foe might thrust him sore;
But he is honest, and plays his tune by the regular score.
You are vexed that I happened to hear only that loud Devil's chorus—
Very well done by the way—which brought all the horror before us,
When you had hoped to have only the lyric of love and endurance,
Swelling out high, at the close, to the joy and the hope and assurance.
But it is all of a piece, love, whether you like it or no,
All of it close-knit together; branched, but the branches grow
Out of the same deep root. I heard but the part of a whole;

I know that the chorus needed the lyric to melt
 the soul,
The lyric implies, too, the chorus; whichever you
 chance to hear,
Always the other is present to fill the heart or the ear.
I am not an unbeliever, love; only I cannot wink
At things I had rather not see, and thoughts I
 had rather not think;
Does it not seem, too, an odd way of quickening
 love and faith,
Picturing wrath that refuses e'en the grim mercy
 of death?
The higher my vision of God, the more I can
 trust and pray;
The better I seem to know him, the broader appears
 the way;
God and charity grow together; and I cannot see
Any dark moment of Time when Hope must cease
 to be.
But will you hear what I thought as that sermon
 thundered on,
With lurid flashes of horror, and God's heart turned
 to stone?

So then he read to me this—"Other-world ballad" he
 calls it—

Of the meek soul that for love heeds not what sorrow befalls it,
Heeds not the bliss and the glory, but longs for them that are lying
Dim in the outer darkness, tossed in the anguish undying.
What can I think of it? what? who will guide me aright—
Me, a weak woman—to walk on in the straight pathway of Light?
Sometimes it rings in my ear as deadly as error could be;
Sometimes I feel in my heart it is true as the gospel to me,
A thing I would do, myself, just then when my Faith is most,
As I remember the love that suffered to save the lost.
But through the years and the ages, the Church, unchanging, cries,
Sad are the foolish virgins, and glad for ever the wise.
Dare I trust my heart's voice against the voice of the whole?
Yet should the roar of the crowd ever drown the true voice of the soul?
O, if clear it were only!

THE SELF-EXILED.

There came a soul to the gate of Heaven
    Gliding slow—
A soul that was ransomed and forgiven,
    And white as snow:
And the angels all were silent.

A mystic light beamed from the face
    Of the radiant maid:
But also there lay on its tender grace
    A mystic shade:
And the angels all were silent.

As sunlit clouds by a zephyr borne
    Seem not to stir,
So to the golden gates of morn
    They carried her:
And the angels all were silent.

"Now open the gate, and let her in,
    And fling it wide,
For she hath been cleaned from stain of sin,"
    St. Peter cried:
And the angels all were silent.

"Though I am cleansed from stain of sin,"
    She answered low,
"I came not hither to enter in,
    Nor may I go:"
And the angels all were silent.

"I come," she said, "to the pearly door.
    To see the Throne
Where sits the Lamb on the Sapphire Floor,
    With God alone:"
And the angels all were silent.

"I come to hear the new song they sing
    To Him that died,
And note where the healing waters spring
    From His pierced side:"
And the angels all were silent.

"But I may not enter there," she said,
    "For I must go
Across the gulf where the guilty dead
    Lie in their woe:"
And the angels all were silent.

"If I enter heaven I may not pass
 To where they be,
Though the wail of their bitter pain, alas!
 Tormenteth me:"
And the angels all were silent.

"If I enter heaven I may not speak
 My soul's desire
For them that are lying distraught and weak
 In flaming fire:"
And the angels all were silent.

"I had a brother, and also another
 Whom I loved well;
What if, in anguish, they curse each other
 In depths of hell?"
And the angels all were silent.

"How could I touch the golden harps,
 When all my praise
Would be so wrought with grief-full warps
 Of their sad days?"
And the angels all were silent.

"How love the loved who are sorrowing,
  And yet be glad?
How sing the songs ye are fain to sing,
  While I am sad?"
And the angels all were silent.

"O clear as glass is the golden street
  Of the city fair,
And the tree of life it maketh sweet
  The lightsome air:"
And the angels all were silent.

"And the white-robed saints with their crowns
  and palms
  Are good to see,
And O so grand are the sounding psalms!
  But not for me:"
And the angels all were silent.

"I come where there is no night," she said,
  "To go away,
And help, if I yet may help, the dead
  That have no day."
And the angels all were silent.

St. Peter he turned the keys about,
    And answered grim;
"Can you love the Lord, and abide without,
    Afar from Him?"
And the angels all were silent.

"Can you love the Lord who died for you,
    And leave the place
Where His glory is all disclosed to view,
    And tender grace?"
And the angels all were silent.

"They go not out who come in here;
    It were not meet:
Nothing they lack, for He is here,
    And bliss complete."
And the angels all were silent.

"Should I be nearer Christ," she said,
    "By pitying less
The sinful living, or woeful dead
    In their helplessness?"
And the angels all were silent.

"Should I be liker Christ were I
    To love no more
The loved, who in their anguish lie
    Outside the door?"
And the angels all were silent.

" Did He not hang on the cursed tree,
    And bear its shame,
And clasp to His heart, for love of me,
    My guilt and blame?"
And the angels all were silent.

"Should I be liker, nearer Him,
    Forgetting this,
Singing all day with the Seraphim,
    In selfish bliss?"
And the angels all were silent.

The Lord Himself stood by the gate,
    And heard her speak
Those tender words compassionate,
    Gentle and meek:
And the angels all were silent.

Now, pity is the touch of God
    In human hearts,
And from that way He ever trod
    He ne'er departs:
And the angels all were silent.

And He said, "Now will I go with you,
    Dear child of love,
I am weary of all this glory, too,
    In heaven above:"
And the angels all were silent.

"We will go seek and save the lost,
    If they will hear,
They who are worst but need me most,
    And all are dear:"
And the angels all were silent.

July, 18—

O my baby, my baby! O sweet sunbeam of bliss!
Brightening my earth for a moment as with a heaven-sealing kiss:
O the sweet smile on his lips! it haunts me by night and day!

All his brief life was a smile that slowly faded away,
As if he just looked in on us here, on his heavenward road,
And saw that we were not meet to rear up the child of God.
Sometimes I try to think, O what a joy to have given
Child of mine to the host that serve and praise in heaven!
He did not need to be christened, his robes were clean and white,
Touching the earth but a moment, he passed to the realm of light.
Sometimes I shudder to think of the earth and the little grave
Under the great church tower where the budding poplars wave.
O my baby, my baby! whether in heaven or there,
Why am I here, and my baby left with no mother's care?
I thought I was dying at one time—would I were dying to-day;
O my baby, how could the Father take thee away?

August, 18—

Winnie has come: my husband thought it might cheer me a bit,
Having an old friend near me, clever and sparkling with wit,
Sharing old memories with me, full of the gossip of town—
The last new book or picture, or fashion of bonnet or gown.
And she was nice, at first, with her chatter about the old times,
When we were schoolmates, and sauntered under the oaks and limes,
And heard the hum of the bees, and the hum of our future in them,
Or watched the swift, brown squirrels climbing the grey beech-stem;
Bright little pictures she cut me out of the old school-world—
All about how we were dressed, and drilled, and scolded, and curled,
And lectured; and then she knows where all the girls have gone—
This with her husband to India, that to New Zealand alone,

Trusting to pick up a husband somewhere away in the bush,
Or, maybe, to set up a school, or to open a shop at a push.
May Grant, the wildest of us, has married a low-church vicar,
Who holds by the orthodox faith, and port as the orthodox liquor;
While Helen, her sister, is all for chasubles, roods, and stoles,
Liftings and bowings, and Catholic manner of saving souls;
Elphie Deering has sold herself to a widower,
And drives in her carriage past his son who had courted her;
Others are strumming pianos, or working in Berlin wools
Pictures of foolish youths for catching the youthful fools;
Lizzie Morrit is dead—she was jilted by a dragoon,
When all her fortune appeared to be railway shares in the moon.
Winnie is clever, but sharp and sarcastic; and lays herself out
To please the men by her wit, which she scatters like sparks about;

No matter who may smart, if only herself may shine
With her spirits unflagging, that sparkle and gleam like wine.
I do not quite like her way with my husband; but all the same
I laugh, and she does me good, and I really am glad that she came.

September, 18—

Surely Winnie is changed; we ne'er had been friends together,
Had she always been ready to sting like a wasp in October weather.
I think there is hardly a name she has not some story about—
Of all that we knew long ago—a story suggesting a doubt.
Each face that I used to remember as beaming with kindly light,
Is smirched with something or other, and no one escapes her spite.
Sneering with scornful laughter, turn wherever she may,
All the glory is dimmed of all that come in her way;

She creeps on the noblest natures stealthily as a cat,
Now with a bite of venom, and now with a wanton pat,
Leaving them not till crushed. And one thing I cannot abide,
The way that she flatters my husband even when I am beside,
Now flopping down on her knees, and staring up in his face,
Clasping her hands, and feigning an ecstacy quite out of place;
Pumping up tears at his pathos, or sighing with heaving breast,
Or giggling and clapping her hands when his humour is wickedest.
He is weak enough to believe her, which makes me colder in praise,
And I care for poetry less than I ever did all my days.
She flatters him daily with words that are silky and soft and sleek,
And no true wife can be pleased when seeing her husband weak.

'Tis growing quite dreadful to hear her now and then, when she speaks
Jauntily of a Faith that needs no God, nor seeks

To trace his work on the earth, or follow his way
    on high,
Noting his glorious footprints clear in the starry sky;
For Nature has in herself the reason for all that is,
And God is an unscientific, needless hypothesis,
Like witches, ghosts, and miracles—dreams of the
    slumbrous night
Which the great dawn of reason has driven away
    with its light!

Thereto my husband made answer—and O I was
    proud and glad;
"Look you, Miss Winnie," he said, "it's your
    method of science that's bad;
Good for its own end, of course; but here it is
    clearly at fault;
God is not found by the tests that detect you an
    acid or salt.
While you search only for secrets that process of
    science sets free,
Nothing you'll find in the world, but matter to
    handle or see.
Here is a book I am reading now; what can your
    method find there?
Boil it, or burn it, dissect it, let microscope scan
    it with care;

What does it show you but paper and ink and
    leather and thread,
All made of chemical simples that, no doubt, you
    have in your head?
But where is the thought, which is all the end and
    use of the book,
And which flows on through its pages clear to my
    mind as a brook
Rippling and singing sweet music to him that hath
    ears to hear?
Have you an acid will test it? a glass that will
    make it all clear?
Or scalpel to cut it? And yet paper and leather and ink
All are but trash, if I find not the thought which
    the writer can think.
What, now, if spirit and God are the thought which
    is written out plain
On the great page of the world, and your method
    of seeking is vain?

October, 18—

I'll not bear this any longer. I know that his heart
    is mine;
But in my house no girl shall make my life sicken
    and pine

When dead—which may be soon—they may do
   what they list; I shall be
With my sweet baby, who now smiles out of the
   darkness on me;
My baby, whose soft little hands pull steadily
   at my heart,
To think of the better land, and cleave to the
   better part.
But this is my home while I live, and none shall
   bring trouble to it;
And he is my own while I live, and she, with
   her saucy wit,
Shall not come between him and me. He cares
   not for her in the least;
If she respected herself she might see that the
   west and the east
Are not more sundered than he from a woman who
   stings and pricks;
He laughs at her sallies of wit, but he sees through
   all of her tricks.
I know what is due to a wife; she thinks me a
   poor, silly fool,
But I can be dignified too, and I don't mean to
   sit down and pule.
Only last evening my ring slipped from my finger,
   and ran

Under her chair—my finger is thin and wasted and wan—
And picking it up, she put it, before my eyes, on her own,
Bidding him look how it fitted her, tight to the joint and the bone,
Just as if meant for her hand. And this was my marriage ring!
How can she sit by my fire, and smile in my face and sting?
O it is dreadful, a woman who has innuendoes and arts,
And looks so simple and sweet, while she knows she is breaking hearts.
Yet I heed not her sneering; but O to be once more alone,
To lay my head on his shoulder, and thrill at the old true tone
Of love that cherished me once, ever petting his fond little wife,
And making a nest for me, rounded of all the angles of life.
Not that I care for petting—I'm not of the March-blossom kind,
Best in its velvet-sheath wrapt up from the blustering wind;

Rough weather I could bear, if only his heart
   were true
Unto the love he once bore me, and unto the
   God he once knew.

That is what troubles me most. The time was I
   prayed him to read
Daily the Book where my soul found help in my
   sorest need,
Light when my day was dark, and strength to my
   fainting will,
Comfort in time of trouble, and healing from
   every ill.
Now there is nothing I dread so much as a text
   from him,
It is as if all the old stars of heaven were changed
   and dim,
Were not in their old places, and had not the
   same clear sense,
Nor dropt on my spirit the dews which gave
   it a gladness intense,
Changed is the meaning of all, though he keeps to
   the words and names;
They are new pictures that look now out of the
   antique frames;

They are new words that he sings now to the old
    tunes I know;
And strange is the taste of the streams now that in
    the old channels flow.
"Lo! as the rod of Aaron," he says, "to minds
    perplexed
The critical art brings water e'en out of the flintiest
    text,
Clears a way through the desert, and gives to us
    angels' bread,
And quickens anew to life the Faith that was well-
    nigh dead."
But when I'm fain to learn the faith he is fain to
    boast,
O but it seems like another God speaking to men
    not lost;
No more the gate is strait, nor heaven is hard
    to win,
No more the world is fallen, nor death the wages
    of sin—
No more is there a curse now crucified on the tree—
No more any Redeemer, nor ransom paid for me.
Nothing is as it used to be; nothing is what it
    seems;
Nothing says what it used to say; and the old
    Faiths are all dreams;

Blindly the saints read the Scriptures, and like dotards obeyed them
They've taken away my Lord, and I know not where they have laid him.
Now when I say this to him, he laughs in his good-humoured way,
Putting me off with a jest, as one with a child might play,
Which is not fair to his wife, however silly I be,
And I am no fool, although I be not so clever as he.
But Winnie, seeing me vexed thus, silently smiles where she sits,
Turning her eyebrows up, and sharpening her scornful wits,
Adding perhaps, by-and-by, "Ye buried your Lord in a creed,
Dark as the Golgotha tomb, and there he lay dead, indeed;
Should you complain that he is not there for you still to embalm
With unguents and spices, the while ye praise your dead Christ in a psalm?
If there's a chance for your gospel to live, which I very much doubt,
It is in this new resurrection the critics would fain bring about,

Laying aside the grave-clothes,—dogma, miracle, myth,
All the dust that the ages have covered his glory with,—
That we may look on the simple man as he lived and died,
Loved and loving and worshipped, and hated and crucified."
So does she cap his wild words with others more wild, and a sneer
Hardens her voice as she speaks, and grates on my heart while I hear.

November, 18—

Winnie has left us at length. I had some trouble about it;
He laughed at her flattery, vowing he hardly could live now without it,
Called her a nice little goose, his Caberfae, with the head,
Brown, of a startled deer just raised from its ferny bed;
And not a thing would he do, and never a word would he say;
It was no business of his; the girl might go or stay;

He would have nothing to do with it; women had
 ways of their own,
No man could venture on trying, of letting their
 wishes be known.
He trusted I did not think his heretic heart was smit
By a girl, because her tongue had a trick of heretical
 wit;
Sure, he was sound in heart, whatever his head
 might be;
And if not very devout, he was devoted to me;
And held to the saying of Paul as the strong hope
 of his life,
That maybe the faithless husband was saved by the
 faith of his wife.
That is the way that he speaks now, always with
 some poor jest,
Leaving a text in the mouth with a strange and
 a bitter taste.
So he left me that morning. O how my heart beat
 wild!
As I went into my room, and prayed to be kept
 meek and mild,
Speaking the truth in love; and I said to myself a
 psalm
That nerved my soul to be patient, and dignified
 too and calm.

Hardly I know what followed. I meant to be firm, but kind,
And for her own sake tell her the thing that was in my mind;
But on the hint of it only, Winnie broke out in her wrath,
Scornful, vowing that I had all along darkened her path,
Made her life fruitless, and that she laughed at my pious advice;
I was but a watery saint, and lapt in a fool's Paradise;
And she could shatter my baby-bliss, if she cared to do it.
O how she pitied my husband! mated, and now, too, he knew it,
Wived by mistake, with one who was wife of his weakness only,
Hardly a housekeeper even, and leaving his intellect lonely,
Having no part in his genius, meeting no play of his wit,
Standing outside of his true life, only a drag upon it!
Vain and weak as he was, had he met but a woman of mind

He yet might have run in the race, but now he is left far behind.
Thus she broke out in wrath, and packing her boxes the while,
Stole a look as she stabbed me, hiding a venomous smile,
Furtive; but I was heedless of all that she said about me,
Till this slighting of him made me wroth as a wife should be.
Pity I lost my temper; but, all the same, truly I would
Lose it to-morrow again if they say of him aught but good.
Altogether it was a weary and heartless day,
But there is light towards evening, and peace, too, for she is away.

BOOK THIRD.

Winifred Urquhart, Materialist.

AT "Prinkle's Establishment,
   On principles strictly religious,
For finishing girls," I spent
   A year in a manner egregious;
'Twas a school of the calender kind,
Meant to put a fine gloss on the mind.

It was there I met Hilda Dalguise,
   And thought her enchantingly fair,
With drops of blue heaven for her eyes,
   And bands of sunbeams for her hair,
And the form of a dainty, round dove
Just made for soft touches of love.

I was not of the gushing-girl sort;
   My soul with ambition was fired,
My tongue something sharp at retort,
   And the people were few I admired:
And I know I detested a saint
More than gambling and powder and paint.

Yet I once had a fit of devotion,
   And worked in the Sunday school,
And whipt up a frothy emotion,
   And prayed, and behaved like a fool;
Till my eyes were opened to see
I was growing a small Pharisee.

But with Hilda I felt I could sit
   All the day, just stroking her hair,
Now to smile at her sweet lack of wit,
   Now to kiss her, for love, anywhere,
To pat her soft hand, or be near
The pink, pearly shell of her ear.

Sweet-breathed as a baby, her mind
   Smelt all of the mother's milk still—
Infant prayers, childish hymns, and the blind,
   Pretty faiths they are fain to instil;
And she seemed, in her white, fluffy dress,
Like a bird I must stroke and caress.

MATERIALIST.

I pitied the beautiful child,
   Knowing life as I thought that I did,
With her pure soul as yet undefiled,
   Always doing the thing she was bid,
And believing all hearts were as true
As the one little heart that she knew.

I was just a year older than she,
   But twenty years older in thought:
She hardly knew more than the bee
   That wots where the honey is got,
Nor dreams that the great purple bell
Has poison hid in it as well.

Yet now I'm not sure that I knew
   So very much more than she did:
There's an instinct for all that is true,
   And for all by wise Nature forbid,
Which is deeper than such wit as then
I had gathered of life and of men.

I was young, and I thought myself old;
   A fool, and conceited me wise;
I ran my crude thoughts in a mould
   That shaped the crude thoughts into lies
With a kind of Byronic belief
In a world full of baseness and grief.

How much I have lived since then!
  What rubs I have gotten and given!
Some whine for their childhood again,
  Some pine for the quiet of heaven:
But my tent, I have no mind to strike it;
'Tis a nice, wicked world, and I like it.

Old Prinkle I took for a prude,
  With her hands in her black thread-mits,
Chap-fingered, and painfully good,
  Yet half-scared out of her wits;
And at first I could not make out
What troubled a soul so devout.

'Twas not the mere burden of care
  For a score of commonplace girls,
Whose manners and dresses and hair,
  Their finger-nails, teeth, and their curls,
With their morals and dinners and laughter,
'Twas her calling in life to look after.

But parents and guardians then wanted,
  For girls at a "Finishing School,"
The old wine of Faith well decanted
  Into flasks which must also be full
Of the world, and of woman's ambition
To better her single condition.

So she had to be worldly-wise,
   And train us for "marrying well;"
And she had to put on a disguise,
   And warn us of Death, too, and Hell;
For the earthly young soul must be given
At least a top-dressing of Heaven.

'Twas against the grain, I admit,
   For she'd fain have been honest and true;
She had neither much culture nor wit,
   She was simply a woman that knew
About womanly ways and things,
Such as colours and dresses and rings.

A good soul, kindly and just,
   But timid, and living in ways
She would never have chosen, but must,
   If she meant to live out all her days
In the highly respectable station
Of finishing sound education.

Not a person to train the young mind,
   For she was not at all intellectual,
And oft her religion would find
   All its efforts were quite ineffectual
To fix her stray thoughts on devotion.
Or show the least touch of emotion.

Thus, when sermon was over at noon
   On Sunday, she'd question us on it;
But her speech would wander off soon
   To a ribbon, a gown, or a bonnet—
Or anything pretty or new
She had seen in the minister's pew.

She used to bubble and bell
   About ladylike manners and ways
In soft purling accents that well
   Suggested her own brighter days;
Then sighed and looked timid about,
As if sure that she should be found out.

And the terror that haunted her so
   Was fear of the Governess, Lane,
Who was dismal and dreary as snow
   When it thaws in a drizzle of rain,
And sharp-eyed, and wanted the school,
And held our dear Prinkle a fool.

Lane had laws for all that we did,
   And for every hour of the day;
This and that we were strictly forbid,
   So and so we were always to say;
And we lived, like nuns in their cells,
'Mid an hourly ringing of bells.

We never did any great wrong,
   Such as schoolboys would do on a hint;
And therefore she had to be strong
   On the tithing of anise and mint;
And taught us to wet our hard pillows
At the lightest of light peccadilloes.

O the old-maiden morals we had,
   So scrupulous, prim, and demure!
What the decalogue never forbade
   Our consciences could not endure:
But life was so low-pitched and sad,
It was quite a relief to be bad.

Then, the wearisome lessons!—the proper,
   Dull prose that we read every day,
Which felt as if boiled in a copper
   To take all the flavour away!
The colourless paragraphs writ
Without reason or fancy or wit!

Yet the poems were worse; they were so
   Lack-a-daisical pretty-sublime,
Spurting upward in little jets d'eau
   To fall with a musical chime;
And we mouthed the sweet verses, Good heavens!
How we mouthed, all at sixes and sevens!

Then the darning and hemming and stitching,
  The broidery and the brocade,
The Berlin-wool figures bewitching,
  And the wonderful trees that we made,
Like green triangles in bloom
Stuck hard on the stick of a broom!

And the scales that we practised for hours,
  Till we hated the sight of the keys!
And the evenings when, ranged out like flowers,
  We had our æsthetical teas,
With music, charades, and advices,
While the parents had biscuits and ices!

French was taught by a starved refugee
  Who had hurled at all tyrants defiance;
And a student, who stormed like the sea,
  Administered globules of science
Well wrapt up in texts to make sure
That the bane should have always its cure.

And thus we were "finished" at last
  On principles strictly religious,
Made ready "to come out" and cast
  Our lines in the ocean prodigious;
And begin the true business of life,
To find some one in want of a wife.

I do not blame Prinkle the least—
   She did what they asked her to do;
They did not wish knowledge increased
   Of the wise and the right and the true;
But they would have a gloss of devotion
On girls who had not a notion,

Except just to marry and dress,
   And to see to their cooks and their dinners,
And live on in soft idleness,
   And on Sunday to call themselves sinners,
And be mothers, ere long, of more fools
To be sent to more "Finishing schools."

They were all odious girls, except Hilda;
   And she was a saint, and a pest
To Julia, Maria, Matilda,
   Amelia, Joan, and the rest;
For her conscience was sure to forbid
Many things that we all of us did.

I never liked saints, as a rule,
   Always flapping their texts in your face,
With warnings of sorrow and dule
   To be dreed in that sulphurous place;
Meanwhile they do no good in this,
As they strain at their glamour of bliss.

But Hilda you could not help loving—
   She was not too prosily pious;
And often our ways disapproving,
   Yet she always stood faithfully by us;
And did not pretend to condemn
Earthly things while she coveted them.

She was not at all clever, except
   That she warbled a song like a bird;
You'd have sat through a whole night, and wept
   In a trance of delight, as you heard
The thrill of that exquisite strain,
Like the nightingale's lyrical pain.

Why do I dwell on all this,
   Recalling those tender, low notes?
And why would I give for one kiss
   Of her lips all my long-treasured thoughts?
Pshaw! who ever yet understood
The why of each whimsical mood?

Besides, it's not true; it is only
   A waft of old sentiment blown
O'er my mind, as I sit rather lonely
   Recalling the days that are gone;
But now is far better than then,
For I live in the thoughts of great men.

When I left old Prinkle's I said,
   "Life is good, and I'll seek my good in it;
'Twill go hard if my hand and my head
   Cannot work for success there, and win it;
But I have not much beauty to boast,
I shall ne'er be a "belle" or a "toast."

So I felt as I turned from my glass,
   Having looked at the brown little features;
The eyes and the forehead might pass,
   For they were an intelligent creature's;
But the mouth had a sneer rather bitter,
When a young-lady simper were fitter.

But my brains I could trust to for thinking,
   My fingers were clever to write,
And thus when my heart was half sinking,
   It rose again higher in might;
And I vowed that I would not be sold
For treasures of silver and gold.

I do not affect to despise
   The riches that make a full life,
With pictures and books and fair eyes,
   Beaming on you, of mistress or wife;
Were I man, I would purchase, of course,
A mansion, a maid, and a horse.

But it's not the same thing to be sold,
   And, perhaps, to be laid on the shelf,
As it is to have and to hold
   These chattels and goods for yourself;
And, besides, I was tired of the way
Men talked, who had nothing to say.

So I gave up the young-lady life,
   The novels, the calls, and the moping,
And the hope to be somebody's wife,
   And the cherished girl-dream of eloping,
Or doing some thing that would ring
Unlike the dull commonplace thing.

I said, Men are stronger than we,
   Though our minds be as subtle as theirs;
For they train the high Reason to see,
   While we put on fantastical airs,
And are fain to look silly, although
Our folly has cunning below.

But I would be true to my sex,
   Would learn with the boldest to think,
Would grapple with things that perplex,
   Would stand on the verge and the brink
Where the seen and the unseen are met,
There to gather what truth I could get.

MATERIALIST.

I had "finished" my education,
   But I found it was now to begin;
For formless and void as creation,
   With the wan, diffuse light breaking in
On the first day of darkness, I knew
Neither what nor how I should do.

So I read from morning till night,
   Brows knit, and with resolute brain,
Till darkness turned slowly to light;
   Yet it came with an aching pain,
For I passed not a word or a jot,
Till it gave up its treasure of thought.

Yet vague and unguided, I missed
   The right path among many ways,
And found myself folded in mist
   Of a dim metaphysical haze,
Till I went up to town, and began
The true science-study of man.

Then the first thing I learnt was, to know
   I had everything yet to learn—
To begin with the taproots that grow
   In the life we can faintly discern,
And trace from the great mother-earth
The growth of our thought and our worth.

It was to an uncle I went,
   A learned physician in town,
Whose evenings of leisure were spent
   In converse with men of renown,
Who joined in a happy alliance
Of politics, letters, and science.

They talked of the small and the great,
   They spoke of the near and the far,
They searched the dim secrets of Fate,
   They traced through the fire-mist and star
The growth of the marvellous Whole,
And birth of the mind and the soul.

They asked for no God to explain,
   They asked but slow shaping of time
To account for the thought in the brain,
   And the conscience of duty and crime,
And the rich, varied life of the creature,
With its changes of organ and feature.

What a world of high wonder was this,
   Growing all out of atoms in motion!
Crowned at length with the glory and bliss
   Of life in the earth and the ocean!
And all by the pure force of law,
Without error or failure or flaw!

So I turned to hard study of science—
  I had tasted it mixed up with creed,
But I broke up that foolish alliance,
  Seeking truth, and the truth does not need
Poor safeguards of faith to secure
That the heart shall be humble and pure.

Truth only is good for the soul,
  Truth only is safe to pursue,
And Truth will her secrets unroll
  But to him who is fearless and true,
And will search out the fact with his test,
And bow where the reason is best.

I had the clear courage of truth,
  And plunged into Häckel at once;
The way was not easy and smooth
  As they make ways in England and France:
But then it was thorough, and that
Was the end I was fain to be at.

How I toiled now that I had the key,
  And gathered up fact and example!
How the world opened up unto me
  As knowledge grew lucid and ample!
I hewed through the jungle a way
From the dark into clearness of day.

All realms of dear nature I sought,
 Far and near, both the vast and minute,
What from depths of the sea had been brought,
 What had lain in the rocks at the root
Of the hills, and the dead and alive
From the lair and the nest and the hive.

Girls called with their mothers to see
 The treasures my patience had stored,
And talked with a simper to me
 Of the wonderful works of the Lord,
And the beautiful butterfly wings,
And the fishes and insects and "things."

They knew not the thoughts that I thought,
 They dreamed not the visions I saw,
They wist not that, still as I wrought
 In the footsteps of infinite law,
Their creeds seemed as vanishing cloud
Which had wrapped the dead mind in a shroud.

How I laughed at their priests, now I knew
 The high priests of nature serene,
Who sought but the clear and the true,
 And the law which for ever hath been,
And scorned every meaningless phrase
Where a lie lay, perdue, in a haze.

MATERIALIST.

I thought how they spent their rich lives,
   Sweeping heaven for lost links in the stars,
Or brooding o'er bees in their hives,
   Or watching the ants in their wars,
Or peering with keen microscope
Where the vibriole whirls in the drop,

Or freezing through chill Arctic winters,
   Ice-bound in the Polar sea,
Or daring wild beasts and adventures
   For a tropical bird or a tree;
While the vicar grows wheezy and fat,
And the minister sleek as a cat.

The apostles and martyrs, I said,
   Of our new modern world are these;
They have struggled and suffered and bled,
   They have sought neither honour nor ease,
But they lead the great march in the van
Of progress and freedom for man.

Facts, ordered and tested with skill,
   They gather, which surely declare
The law which all beings fulfil,
   And how through all ages they fare
From the cell to the organ, and soar
Ever up from the less to the more.

How my bosom swelled high as I rose
    To the height of that formative thought,
And saw the dim fire-mist disclose
    The worlds when as yet they were not,
And the life which was one day to flower
From its subtle and manifold power.

What a poem of nature was there!
    How it linked all being in one,
The tree and the bird in the air,
    And the lichen that tints the grey stone,
And the coral that builds the wild reef,
With man and his glory and grief!

They tell of a Fall bringing thorns,
    They talk of a Lost Paradise,
They prate of a devil with horns
    Ever plotting some wicked device,
They will have it that death entered in,
When Eve ate the apple of sin.

But truth, searching out the old myths,
    Sees growth evermore going on,
And, breaking old fetters like wyths,
    Finds death when no sin could be done;
Not a lapse, but a law of survival,
Where the fittest treads down its weak rival.

MATERIALIST.

Poor fools! we keep wrapping our minds
   In the old tattered rags of the Jew,
And shiver and shake as fresh winds,
   Cloud-driving, make larger our view;
And we draw our rags closer about,
Though the faith be as chill as the doubt.

But this is the truth that alone
   Can save from the fever and fret,
That the high law changeth for none,
   That it holds all enmeshed in its net,
And that life and death and endeavour
Ever have been, and shall be for ever.

And life is the fuller for each
   Whose death makes it richer for all;
Immortal the race, bound to reach
   Ever onward; but singly we fall
Into dim silent graves on the road,
As the weary soul lays down its load.

But the dim, silent graves by the way
   Are the footprints of progress for man;
And we are not so selfish as they
   Who only will die, if they can
Hope to knit up again from the dead
The old tangled hank of their thread.

A nobler faith ours; for we know
   That the organs, dissolving for ever,
Shall paint the spring-flowers as they grow,
   But we shall return again never;
And we grudge not the life that shall give
Larger life unto them that do live.

We work for the good of the whole;
   We work, and the rest cometh soon;
We work with no fear for the soul;
   We work in a light as of noon;
And the peace, by-and-by, shall be ours
Of the long drowsy grass and the flowers.

We have faith; we have passed from the mist
   Of doubt and denial and fear
Into high and calm realms that are kissed
   By the sunshine of certainty clear;
And the great thought of duty is freed
From the dross of a self-seeking creed.

O the gladness I had as this grew
   Into clearness now day after day!
At first, I shrank back from the new,
   Startling thoughts that it brought into play.
And the courage of truth that it needed,
And the loneliness as it proceeded.

But plunging, at length, in the tide,
   I flung off the shivering fit
As the current swept stately and wide,
   And cast myself wholly on it;
And slowly the loneliness found
A genial life gathering round.

No shade of a drear world to come
   Lay dismally now on my earth;
No fruitless regretting struck dumb
   The laughter of light-hearted mirth;
I had conscience to prompt me, of course,
But never to sting with remorse.

The needle that points to the Pole
   Does not prick the poor sailor who errs
As the big billows tumble and roll,
   Or the long swell throbs and stirs;
But simply, by night and by day,
The needle just tells him the way.

Even so was I merry and glad
   As I walked in the law and the light;
And so was I not very sad
   When I wandered at times from the right;
And ever the needle was true,
And showed me the thing I should do.

I did not sin and repent,
  And then fall a sinning again,
As if conscience were properly meant
  To keep up a blister of pain;
But I tried to walk in the truth,
And to lose not a joy of my youth.

They say that a vanishing creed
  Makes the heart very weary and sad,
That its wounds must be open and bleed,
  That its ways must be evil and bad;
But I ne'er was in happier mood,
Nor so true to the right and the good.

Well; just then, I heard, by the way,
  That Hilda was wedded, and wrote
A well-meaning letter to say
  How it pleased me to think of her lot,
Reminding her, too, like a fool,
Of a promise she gave me at school.

I offered a visit, to share
  In the joy of a life that I loved;
But I fancy she did not just care
  To be kissed and "honeyed" and "doved"
Before me, but would be alone
Till the honeymoon sweetness was gone.

So she put me off for a year
  With this and the other excuse,
Not one of them simple and clear,
  But all of them shifty and loose;
And yet when she finally sent,
And asked me to visit, I went.

Then I dropt on a scene quite idyllic,
  A nook of the old paradise—
A rose-embowered cot on a hillock,
  With a garden sunny and nice,
And my saint and her poet too yawning
At the commonplace life that was dawning.

I cannot describe; but I know
  The country was not picturesque;
The granite lay barren below,
  And a broad moor, as flat as my desk,
Stretched inwards, and down to the sea
There was hardly a bush or a tree.

But inside was pretty enough;
  The rooms all so fresh and so sweet—
Not a jar, or a word that was rough,
  Not a thing but was dainty and neat,
And Hilda so gentle and still,
Though the meek little fool had a will.

I did not much take to her now;
  She seemed to be stunted in growth,
A pale, sickly bloom on a bough,
  A flat, tasteless thing in the mouth;
A chaste, cold, passionless ghost,
Weeping much for a babe she had lost.

I tried to cheer her a bit,
  But she did not interest me;
She never did smack much of wit,
  But now she was dull as the sea
When the east wind blows its grey haar,
As it moans on the sand and the bar.

It was always that baby, forsooth!
  As if blossoms had never been nipt,
As if lambs never died in their youth,
  As if no other babies had slipt
Away to the peace of the worm
From life, and its trouble and storm.

But her Poet was really a man;
  Not a clinker only of rhymes,
But one who could thoughtfully scan
  The world, and the men, and the times,
And see their meanings, and sing
The vision of life which they bring.

MATERIALIST.

He was not the least of a saint;
  But worked, with a patient might,
In the Artist's unconstraint,
  With the Artist's frank delight
In the quaint and the unexpected
Moulds which his thought selected.

Still mooning in twilight dim,
  His humour was just to croon
Any song that was pleasing to him,—
  Fresh words to the old, old tune,
And his thought was but half-expressed
In the manner of mirthful jest.

He had ever a kindly touch
  In his quips and tricks and mocks,
But playfully hinted much
  Abhorred by the orthodox;
Yet he trifled, when he should have smote
With the sharp battle-axe of his thought.

He was vain too—he was a poet—
  You hardly could flatter enough;
And you did not need not to show it,
  He could swallow the rankest stuff;
Though he laughed at himself as he did it,
Yet next time he did not forbid it.

He never was thorough or strong,
  But fanciful only, and odd,
Never sure of the right and the wrong,
  And he still would believe in a God,
And talked, with a vague kind of beauty,
Of the soul, and its hope and its duty.

But that is the way with most men;
  They dare not much more than to doubt;
They dare not, one man out of ten,
  To think their thought thoroughly out;
The practical plucks at their sleeve,
And they're frightened to shock and to grieve.

I played on his foible awhile;
  And made myself useful to him,
Now giving a touch to his style,
  Now setting his papers in trim,
Now glancing at nature to show it
In lights that are new to the poet.

But he never could cast off the shapes
  Of shallow and silly romance—
The frost-work that dims, as it drapes,
  Our window, and hides from our glance
The beauty of truth, and the story
Of life with its wonder and glory.

The poet will still be a child,
   And will curtain the sun to his slumbers;
At the great chemic laws he half smiled,
   And laughed at the rhythm of its numbers,
And joked at the glass or the knife
Detecting the secret of life.

Yet I liked him; but Hilda grew jealous—
   She cared not for verse or for rhyme,
Except as the wind in the bellows,
   That brightened her hearth for the time;
Yet she would have the whole of his heart,
And was touchy and sniffy and tart.

And one night he read us a ballad,
   As we sat the work-table around,
Which his humour composed like a salad
   Of any green stuff that it found
Cropping up on a fanciful soil,
And he mixed it with wit as with oil.

I am sure that I have it somewhere,
   For I wrote it all down the next day:
Here it is; and a sorry affair
   It is to have made such a fray:
Yet 'twas like him, it must be confessed
To make sentiment flower out of jest.

JUDAS ISCARIOT.

The very Prince of Darkness
  Came once to Heaven's gate,
Where Peter and the angels
  Talk together as they wait;
And he brought with him a spirit
  In a very dismal state.

Then Satan: "I'm in trouble,
  And come here to get advice;
I've been going up and down there
  Where you think we are not nice,
And they will not have this fellow
  Among them at any price.

"I took him first to Lamech
  And the bloody race of Cain,
But they rose in flat rebellion,
  That so mean a rogue should gain
A place with gallant fellows
  Who in simple wrath had slain.

"Then I thought of those wild Herods
　With their burning diadem,
And their spirits, ever haunted
　By the babes of Bethlehem:
But they would not have the traitor
　Coming sneaking among them.

"After that I looked to Ahab,
　And the panther Jezebel;
But she sprang up like a fury,
　'It were shame unspeakable
To lodge a half-hanged felon
　Where a queen of men must dwell.'

"I'm afraid there's not a corner
　Into which they'll let him in;
The common rogues are furious
　To confound them with his sin,
And my people are excited,
　And the place is full of din."

Then Peter: "Traitor Judas,
　Thou hearest what he says,
How the murderers and demons
　Abhor thee and thy ways,
Thou betrayer of the Holy,
　Who the Ancient is of days."

Then Judas answered meekly :
"Yea, Peter, they are right ;
Cain and Lamech, Ahab, Herod,
 They were godless men of might,
But not so vile as I am—
 O they loathe me, and are right.

" Jezebel that slew the prophets,
 Fawned not on the life she stole ;
Ahab only smote the servants,
 Not the Lord who bare our dole ;
There should be a hell expressly
 For my miserable soul.

"Let my name be named with horror,
 Let my place be wrapt in gloom,
Let me even be hell's lone outcast,
 With a solitary doom—
I that kissed Him, and betrayed Him
 To the cross, and to the tomb."

Then Satan : " There's the mischief,
 He goes whining like a saint ;
I could keep my people quiet,
 But he'd have them penitent.
It's as bad as if a parson
 Made their very hearts grow faint."

But, as Peter looked on Judas,
    Sunk in utter misery,
Lo! there rose before his vision,
    A grey morning by the sea,
And a weary, broken spirit
    On the shores of Galilee.

"O once, too, I despairèd,
    For my Lord I had denied,
And once my heart was breaking,
    For I cursed Him, and I lied;
I did not slay myself, but yet
    I wished that I had died.

"Leave thy burden with me, Satan,
    He is not too bad for me;
He will get 'his own place' duly,
    And it is not mine to be
A breaker of the bruised,
    Or the judge of such as he."

I praised it; but she gazed to heaven
    As if he had sinned the great sin
Which is not atoned or forgiven,
    And no touch of pity can win,
And nobody knows what it is,
But her soul sat and trembled for his.

She said, "It was jesting with sin,
    And nothing but grief came of that;
Few may play with the devil, and win,
    Whatever the game they are at;
And Heaven was not surely a place
For one who despaired of its grace."

I said, "It was quaint and bizarre,
    And its humour was what I liked best;
And I thought they were much on a par,
    Who spoke, or in earnest or jest,
Of the souls of the bad or the just,
When their brains were a small pinch of dust."

She fired up at that; "Did I mean
    That the soul was all one as the brain?
Had I only a faith in the Seen,
    With its animal pleasure and pain?—
Had I left the old paths that were trod
By the saints, and the true men of God."

I could not help smiling to see
    Her look so bewildered and scared,
When her anger broke out upon me,
    As if I had her husband ensnared
In some terrible plot to disown
All the gods that have ever been known.

"It was I made him mock and blaspheme—
  I who knew no more than the cat!
And her life had been bright as a dream
  Till I came with the dusk like a bat;
For I hated the name of the Lord,
Whom every true woman adored.

"I was impious, false, and cruel;
  I could sit at her fire and sting;
I would fain rob her life of the jewel
  She prized above everything;
Yet all that she might have forgiven,
But I mocked at her God up in heaven."

Of course, he behaved like a man,
  Tried to soothe her, and smoothe matters down,
And then, backing out of it, ran
  Away to some job of his own;
But he got me persuaded to stay
When I should have at once gone away.

That was weak, I confess; but the place
  Was nice, and his humour was pleasant,
And there was such a light in his face,
  Now and then, when his wife was not present,
That—well, I remained for a time,
Enduring her moods and his rhyme.

But her temper got worse every day;
    She feared me, and her I despised;
And he still let her have her own way,
    Only soothed her, and meekly advised;
So I left them, at last, in a trance
Of piety, love, and romance.

I hear that she blamed me because
    I made myself useful to him;
But what could I do when she chose
    To be distant and silent and prim?
In truth, she was never his mate,
Poor thing! she was only his Fate.

Of course, he was nothing to me;
    He wanted a slave in his wife,
Who should worship him low on her knee,
    And serve with the breath of her life;
And there's nothing I ever abhorred
Like a man for my Master and Lord.

My Master is science divine,
    My Lord is the truth that I seek,
My service is Freedom, and mine
    Was ne'er the poor heart of the meek:
I would lean upon none, for I live
On that which great Nature can give.

MATERIALIST.

Poor Hilda! I give her my pity,
   And I pity her husband still more;
He will rhyme away life in a ditty,
   She will make of her soul a heartsore;
Religion will quarrel in time
With Romance—and he'll put it in rhyme:

And be comforted, too, as he reads
   The tale of his sorrow and grief,
Binding up his poor heart while it bleeds,
   With the balm of a smooth-rhyming leaf;
He will drop for his Hilda a tear,
And gloat o'er his verse for a year.

Now I think of it, somebody said,
   That the crash had come some time ago;
She had either gone off, or was dead,
   And a poem from that was to grow,
Which was certain to touch every heart
With its feeling of fine tragic Art.

If I had not that paper to write
   On the dawning of mind in Moluscs,
And that other to set people right
   On the subject of Molars and Tusks,
I think, I would like just to see
What he says about Hilda and me.

BOOK FOURTH.

Luke Sprott, Evangelist.

EVANGELIST and village smith, a man of good report,
  And cunning among cattle, known to all the country near,
Luke could make the bellows snore, and also painfully exhort,
  And feared the Lord, and had a new religion once a year.

He had been a Chartist leader in his hot and hopeful youth,
  Talking gunpowder and bayonets about the rights of man,
Until he got converted, when he preached about the Truth,
  The Blood and the Atonement, the Covenant and Plan.

Tired of his parish kirk, he tried the Baptists for
  a season,
  Tired of them, and turned a Methodist, recanting
    all the past,
Tired again, and took to shady faiths that shun
    the ways of reason;
  And every change, he vowed, had brought the
    peace of God at last.

And every change had left a stratum of belief on
    him,
  With fossils here of Presbytery, there of his Baptist
    time,
Then traces of the Methodist, and now the foot
    prints dim
  Of reptiles that had sprawled across the later
    mud and slime.

For partly Antinomian now, and partly Manichee,
  He blundered back to church, and deemed that
    he was orthodox,
And stormed at modern thinking as the raging of
    the sea
  That cast up mire and dirt upon the everlasting
    rocks.

And yet his heart was right, although his thought was so confused—
  A tangled knot of broken thrums he could not extricate;
All ordered thought of reason and of science he abused,
  But he was full of pity, and his love was very great.

And because he was so earnest, and because he spoke good words
  Whose meaning none searched nicely, and because he seemed to stir
Serious thoughts in careless hearts, as if he touched their higher chords,
  He was sought, and he was looked to as a chosen minister.

A great broad-headed fellow, working hard through all the week,
  And thinking hard the while he worked upon the fate of man,
He was fain to save the sinner and the erring, and would speak
  A world about the chaff and wheat, and sifting with a fan.

There was a thick husk in his voice that weirdly rose and fell,
  As with a knotted fist he smote upon a horny palm,
And poured his prophet-burden about sin and death and hell,
  Now like tender, pleading Gospel, now like bitter cursing Psalm.

The man had power, for certain, for he had a human heart,
  Gleams of humour, tender touches, too, of pathos, and throughout
A vein of clear sincerity whose might is more than art,
  And the firmness of a soul that had not any wavering doubt.

And when he came about our house, at first, I liked to hear
  His pithy words, good-humoured if you did not say him nay;
And stories of himself that were like flotsam drifting near
  From tempests of an unknown sea whose storms were far away.

He had a keen shrewd humour, but it mostly had
    to do
  With the meaner part of nature, and was blind
    to what is best;
He put his finger on a blot that shamed and
    humbled you,
  And thought he read you truest when you showed
    unworthiest.

Though God was always in his mouth, you did not
    feel the awe
  Which hangs about the Presence when he spoke
    of the Supreme;
He was more at home with Satan; then he spake
    as if he saw;
  But to me his speech of God was like an echo
    or a dream.

And yet I liked him, swinging with long strides at
    gloaming late,
  And stretching his vast limbs beside the blazing
    winter fire,
With pale, lean face, and lanky hair, and speech
    deliberate,
  That never ceased to flood the house, and never
    seemed to tire.

Not that it was good to hear him, for it did not
    raise you higher;
  It showed your baser self, but did not rouse
    the better part ;
He could search the hidden evil, but he never could
    inspire
  Unto any nobler life by his unveiling of the
    heart.

Man was not lovely to him, nor yet lovely was his
    God ;
  The cynic thought breeds mostly bitter faith in
    things divine ;
Who sees no beauty in the soul that bears its
    human load,
  Shall see but little glory where the gods of glory
    shine.

There was humour in his sayings, though he meant
    them not for jest—
  Too earnest he for mirth, except a hard and
    bitter grin ;
Yet his shrewdness had an oddness being quaintly
    oft expressed,
  And I laughed with laugh the keener that I had
    to laugh within.

'Twas something fresh to me, to follow slowly up
    and down
  The windings of his tangled talk, and make the
    thought complete;
I perused him like a volume whose leaves, dog-
    eared and brown,
  Held bits of the rough poetry that lies about
    our feet.

There was a rude ideal which he struggled to attain,
  A poem floating in his mind, but mangled by the
    lack
Of ordered thought to shape the hope, the passion
    and the pain;
  And he blundered into broken paths to shun the
    beaten track.

What puzzled me about him was, to see him still
    so sure,
  So changeful, yet so certain that his way was
    always right;
And that his vision was so dim, although his heart
    was pure,
  And that he could so grossly err, yet be a
    child of light.

I read his meaning partly, as one reads a palimpsest,
  Dimly traced upon the vellum under monkish hymns and prayers
And trumpery tales of wonder; and I understood him best
  When I watched his human kindness taking up our human cares.

He fancied I was smitten with his views, when I was only
  Making him a curious study for the work I had to do,
Just a theme for long reflection, as I sat in silence lonely,
  Shaping out the world around me in the poet's large review.

But I had no right to trifle with the follies of a friend,
  Or to play upon his humour to find matter for a book;
I might have known that that would come to some unhappy end,
  For to toy with human hearts, is more than human hearts will brook.

'Tis the sin of art's fine passion that it only seeks to know,
  Not to perfect, any creature that his lot he may fulfil;
It has charity to bear with any rankest weeds that grow
  Unto any picturesqueness, and to leave them growing still.

Priest and prophet try to save, and so their work is blessed; but mine
  Strove only just to see, and reproduce the picture true,
Making sacrifice of duty for the trimming of a line,
  Heeding not of higher wisdom in the itch for something new.

O my heart and its misgivings! I am never wholly sure.
  Was the art of Greece so perfect that its life was also high?
Is the heavenly vision only seen what time the heart is pure?
  Is the poem but the poet as he dares to live and die?

Could I be a mere onlooker, and yet see what should be seen?
  Standing calmly on the outside, could I paint this life aright?
Nay, that could never come to any perfect fruit, I ween,
  Could yield but sickly blossom nipt by any frosty night.

Better wield a pick or spade, or drive a furrow in the soil,
  Bear a hod, or hurl a barrow among fustian-wearing men,
Win humblest daily bread by daily sweat of honest toil,
  Than live to find in life but stuff for scrawling with a pen!

One evening Luke, as usual, held discourse of human ills,
  And I turned me somewhat weary from his ever-lasting bleat,
Monotonous, like sheep among the solitary hills,
  As he mooned away to Hilda sitting on the window seat.

Something, I know, had fretted me—I cannot now
    say what,
  Only living among dreams, and sitting far into
    the night,
With none to bid good-speed unto the labour I
    was at,
  And a pained, though dumb suspicion that, per-
    haps, I did not right

To peril all the tender bliss of home for such an aim,
  Bred an irritable temper when I was not all
    alone,
And so it fevered me to hear—though they were not
    to blame—
  Her weary stitching needle, and his weary preach-
    ing drone.

He had, somehow, raised the wonder that begets
    a woman's faith,
  The sense of power and mystery that awes her
    with belief;
His God was not the Father that giveth life and
    breath,
  Yet she looked to him for guidance, and for
    comfort in her grief.

Women cling to any spirit that is confident and bold,
  Taking doubt to be a sin, the sign of an untrustful mind;
And I was sure of nought; I saw the shadows round me fold,
  And felt that life was very dark, and I was very blind.

I was not fit to guide her, for myself I could not guide
  Through the valley of the shadow; only groping as I went,
Step by step, and never certain of the shepherd at my side,
  And my soul was often troubled, and my heart was often faint.

But he was sure of all things in earth and hell and heaven,
  Sure that we were devil's children all, and heirs of wrath to come,
Sure that on the bitter cross a sum of ransom had been given
  To purchase men from Satan, or at least to purchase some.

And this so certain dogmatism she took for faith divine,
  Infallible, intrenched within a wall of texts and
    creeds,
And believed in him entirely, while she turned from
    words of mine
  As from henbane, hemlock, nightshade, or other
    deadly weeds.

That night he went on, ceaseless, in his hortatory tone
  Half-saying and half-singing, and I could not
    choose but hear
Broken snatches of his doctrine, like the melancholy
    moan
  Of the wind that in the crannies sounds so dismal to the ear.

LUKE'S DISCOURSE.

It is not our sins that send us there:
  There are sinners as bad in the heavenly choir,
And souls as sweet as the summer air
  Up to their lips in the lake of fire:
Stained with vices, as black as night,
  Some shall be found on the narrow way;
For seen by the Lord from his holy height
  All your virtues are black as they.

It is our unbelief slams the door,
　And rams in the bolt too, right in our face,
But so much the more are our sins, the more
　Glory there is to abounding grace.
What, if one wronged you, meaning it not?
　What, if one hurt you just by a word?
No great credit to wipe that blot,
　Or to forget what you need not have heard.
But if I hate you, make you a liar,
　Slay your dearest, and mock at his name,
O the mercy that rises higher
　The higher the sinner's guilt and blame!

Only believe in the Lamb they slew,
　And in the blood that from Him did flow;
Only believe that He died for you,
　And it shall wash you as white as the snow.
O but the Blood is the life of Faith!
　Even one drop would a world redeem.
Blood on the lintels, and ancient Death
　Passed by the door like a hideous dream;
Blood on his raiment made the Priest
　Holy to stand where the Lord was seen;
Blood on the altars wrath appeased;
　Blood on the sinner, and he is clean.

Science and learning are but snares,
  Reason and knowledge they are traps;
Better lie down with wolves and bears
  Than with critical principles, books, and maps.
Once I starved in the Hebrides,
  Nearly a month, on whelks and clams,
And fish-like birds from the grey salt seas,
  While I tried to think they were beeves and
    lambs :
So is the soul that feeds on stuff
  Reason gives it instead of bread;
So is the man who is swollen with fluff
  Science is fain to put into his head.
These cannot take one sin away,
  Bring no peace to the troubled heart;
As well down on your knees and pray
  To the graven image of heathen art.

Children make-believe anything, whiles
  They have plenty to eat and drink,
Make a grand feast out of slates and tiles,
  And water is wine if you only wink.
O how nicely they carve a stone!
  O how pretty they drink the toast!
This is the shortbread, that the scone,
  There are the platters of boiled and roast!

But let the thirst and hunger come,
  And give them for bread their slates and stones,
And poor little hearts! all their prattle is dumb,
  And make-believe ends in tears and moans.

So is the soul that plays with shams,
  So till there comes an hour of need;
So shall it starve on whelks and clams
  Of rational thought and virtuous deed.
But let him see the guilt and gloom,
  But let him smell the burning lake,
And hear, as it were, the billows boom
  Where is no shore for them to break.
Only the Blood then that atones,
  Only the blood can give him rest:
Hence with your make-believe slates and stones,
  He must have truth, for truth is best.

Hell and the devil (I thought the words
  Came from his lips with a kind of smack,
And round and rich, as the singing birds
  Dwell on a choice note, and call it back)—
Hell and the devil will have their due;
  O you may rush at a ditch or hedge,

And scramble through with a scratch or two,
   And a tattered skirt to the other ledge;
But there's no bottom to yonder pit,
   There is no other side to hell,
There is no make-believe in it,
   And there for ever the faithless dwell.

A terrible picture! aye, and whiles
   I have almost thought that it could not be,
As I looked on the bay with its sunny smiles
   Glinting over the laughing sea.
There the fishermen trim their boats,
   The wives at the door are baiting lines,
Mirth of the children blithely floats
   Up from the beach as they touch the spines
Of round sea-urchin under the dulse,
   Or hunt the crab in the shady pool,
And the small waves beat like a tranquil pulse,
   And the seal comes out of the cavern cool,
Bobbing his head above the sea,
   There where the white gulls dive and swim,
And the swift ships pass like clouds that be
   Hung on the grey horizon dim.
Then I have thought, till my heart grew faint,
   And my head swam with the vision dire:

"O beautiful Earth, is it really meant
   Thou shalt be wrapped in the flaming fire?
These happy homes where I oft have sat,
   These hands I have held in friendly grip,
Those curly children I love to pat,
   Or to press their cheeks with a prayerful lip,
Can they be fated—one of them even—
   Yet in the outer dark to lie,
Far away hid from the glory of Heaven,
   And gnawed by the worm that cannot die?
O the anguish that thought has sent
   Thrilling all through my heart and brain!
And Word and warning and argument
   The Spirit has pleaded with me in vain.
I thought it was righteous to rebel,
   I thought that it was for God I spoke
When I wrestled against the pains of hell,
   Like Jacob, until the morning broke.
But who am I to reject His word
   That tells of the deathless worm and fire?
And where were the mercy of the Lord
   If it plucked not brands from the burning pyre?

Here I broke in, You should have heard your heart,
   for it was true;
   I think it was the voice of God for pity pleading then,

And you have crushed your pity with a text that
    deadened you,
  And texts are meant for quickening all the nobler
    thoughts of men.

He took no notice of my speech; I wot not if he
    heard,
  Because there rose a gust of wind, shrill-whistling
    from the sea;
But by and by there came a lull, and with the
    lull a word
  I was not meant to hear, though it was shrewdly
    meant for me.

Truly you tell me his faith is gone,
  Truly I see only doubting in him:
He has buried the Christ, and sealed the stone,
  And watches all night 'mid the shadows dim,
That none may quicken his soul again,
  That none may quicken his hope anew;
And I have noted the sorrow and pain
  Of the great love that was wasting you.
Lady, as slowly the cloud came down,
  Slowly and coldly the mist was creeping

Over a soul that is dear as your own ;
   And angels were watching with you and weeping.

Yea, I have grieved for him, and I have prayed
   Through the long night, as I watched afar,
Sign of the poor part in life that he played,
   The lamp from his window that gleamed like a star ;
There he is toiling, I said, for a bubble,
   Which when he touches it, shall be no more,
Reaping the harvest of sorrow and trouble,—
   Here I will pray till his labour is o'er :
Long as his lamp burns for folly of fame,
   So long shall mine that his soul I may win ;
Shall he unwearying toil for a name,
   And I grow weary to save him from sin.
Thus have I stormed at the gates of heaven
   All the more that he laughed at me,
Just that his soul might to me be given
   All the more we could never agree.
I see that he mocks me, and flouts me, and jibes
   At all the things that I honour most,
And seeks the lore of the clerks and scribes
   More than the word of the Holy Ghost.

He would put me into a book, I know,
    That wits might crackle their jests so droll,
And laugh at the preaching smith whose blow
    Could smite the iron, and miss the soul,
Yet I have loved him, O so well!
    Yet I have prayed for him, O how long!
But he would risk all the terrors of hell
    For the point of a jest, or the rhyme of a song.
O he is just like a schoolboy that cares
    Only to hear his whip go crack
In the dim streets, and the silent squares,
    While the echo comes ringing back;
High in the heaven he would sit and brood,
    With a flickering smile on his dubious lip;
And down in hell would find some good
    In trying how loud he could crack his whip.

You are wroth with me now, for the truth that I speak;
    You would have me to smile, and beck, and cringe,
And not let the gate of darkness creak,
    But smoothly work on its well-oiled hinge,
And silently close on an erring soul,
    With just a snap when the deed is done;

And then I must whimper and condole,
  With a lying hope that the goal was won,
Although he never had run the race,
  Never so much as made the start.
But I cannot be sweet before your face,
  And false to you in my inmost heart.
Tell me not of his love of truth,
  Kindly spirit, and thoughtful care,
Or the pure love of his noble youth—
  Tell me of faith, if faith be there.
Water the coals, and they will burn,
  Sun-dry the faggot, and it will flame;
So virtue or vice will serve your turn,
  And make you ready for wrath and shame.
Faith alone is the master-key
  To the strait gate and the narrow road;
The others but skeleton picklocks be,
  And you never shall pick the locks of God.

But hush! His thunders are in the heaven,
  Rumbling low through the clouded sky,
Like the roll of wheels that are swiftly driven
  With flames from the whirling tires that fly.
Who knows? They are maybe sent for him
  To clothe his spirit with awe and fear:

Close we the windows and sing a hymn,
   And pray while the Lord is plainly here.
Well to improve the solemn hour,
   Well to smite while the bar is hot;
Surely the Lord is great in power,
   Woe to him that believeth not.

He had been speaking low to her, and wist not I could hear;
   And though I heard I heeded not, my thoughts were so intent
Watching the signs of coming storm that darkled far and near,
   And all his words fell off from me, like arrows blunt and spent.

From every part of heaven the clouds crept, slow, across the sky,
   Black clouds, with lurid edges, and rifts of leaden gray,
And earth lay still and breathless as they mustered there on high,
   Nor lark nor throstle noting the dimly dying day.

Now, all was wrapt in darkness, without twinkling
 of a star,
 And the big thunder-rain came down in sullen
 warning drops;
Beneath the silent trees the silent kine were grouped,
 and far
 The sea moaned, and a shiver passed along the
 tall tree-tops.

And then it burst in fury—rain and hailstones
 mixed with fire,
 And sudden gusts of wind that howled across
 the stony moor,
With awful lulls, and shattering peals that nearer
 grew and higher;
 And one great ball of hissing fire fell almost at
 the door.

A wild, black night of tempest, such as men remem-
 ber long
 In the dull undated life of a sleepy country town,
When forests fell before the wind, streams swept
 off bridges strong,
 And church-towers, lightning-shivered, reeled, and
 then came crashing down.

Awe-stricken, yet entranced, I watched, with tremulous joy, each phase
  And movement as it registered itself upon the mind,
While the strained sense, exulting in the wonder and amaze,
  Jarred at a common sound amid the thunder and the wind.

Thus when I heard his husky voice 'mid nature's grandest tones
  Of so transcendant harmony, for harmony was there
In all the roll of thunder, and the shrieks and wailing moans,
  It smote me like an insult—that suggestion of a prayer.

I did not speak at first; I did but grip his bony wrist
  And whisper to be silent, and led him to his seat,
Imperious in a wrath whose stern resolve was only hissed
  Into his ear; and he was cowed, and sat in silence meet.

Silent only for a little; by-and-by there came a lull,
  And, coughing, he spake something about the wrath of heaven;
Then I said, When God was preaching other sermons sounded dull,
  And I wanted no "improvement" of the lesson He had given.

I said that, for myself, I did not wish to be improved,
  And doubted if he could at all improve the work of God;
But if he thought the wrath of heaven against himself was moved,
  He might pray there like a worm on whom his Deity had trod.

I added that the tempest was a mercy clear to me,
  The very thing I needed for the volume that I wrote;
It came in time precisely, and my book was sure to be
  A great success, with such a glorious picture in the plot.

I had just come to a point where I required a
 thunder-storm,
  And heaven was kind to send it in the very
   nick of time ;
And I was very grateful not to be a trampled
 worm,
  But a favourite of the gods who gave me matter
   for my rhyme.

If the Father cares for sparrows, He may surely
 care for books,
  And send a troubled author storm or sunshine
   which he needs ;
If winds were sent to farmers for the winnowing
 of their stooks,
  Surely poets might get weather for recording of
   His deeds.

And why should men be grateful for a fine potato
 crop,
  Or sunshine for the oats, or rain to make the
   turnips grow,
And thankless for the wholesome books that fruitful
 authors drop,
  Or a publisher's good season up in Paternoster
   Row.

And God was good to me, I said, in gathering his cloud,
  I saw a special providence in letting loose the wind;
That He cared to feed the hungry every pious heart allowed,
  But He must doubly care to feed the hunger of the mind.

The more he stared and gasped at me, the more I pushed him hard;
  Saying, Surely the book-harvest was heaven's peculiar care;
The Church might be God's vineyard, but the verses of the bard
  Were the ripe fruits of his orchard, and the flowers that made it fair;

And novels were the poppies, red and sunny in the field,
  And histories were wholesome oats, and essays were the rich
Clover-fields that fed His kine, and made the butter that they yield,
  While sermons were the small-weeds growing in the hedge or ditch;

And tracts were for his horses, like the vetches and
  the tares
 To be munched up by the bushel, being savourless
  and dry;
But songs were his ripe apples; and his apricots and
  pears
 Were ballads and the lyric strains of love, that
  never die.

I wot not why I chattered so amid the sullen
  lull,
 While the tempest took its breath, and gathered
  for another burst;
It was his face that tempted me, it looked so blank
  and dull;
 And partly I revenged me for his talk with Hilda,
  first.

Because he was a preacher, she had let him say to
  her
 What no one else had dared to say without her
  proud rebuke;
But any thing that called itself a Christian minister
 She heard as she would hearken to the Volume
  of the Book.

Low in my heart I laughed then to see him stare
    and gasp
  At that imagined book for which the thunder had
    been sent,
And at his puzzled horror as I buzzed like stinging
    wasp,
  Too swift for his slow movements, in my wanton
    merriment.

No book then was I writing that needed storm or
    calm,
  Nor could I copy Nature in that hard and soulless
    way,
Barely cataloguing facts, although I heard, as 'twere
    a Psalm
  Of awe-inspiring joy, the grand orchestral thunder
    play.

And truth may lie in laughter too, and wisdom in
    a jest,
  And wit may lend its sparkle to the reverential
    thought;
And solemn fools shall talk to you their wisest and
    their best,
  And leave you very weary with the nothing you
    have got.

At length he rose in anger, would not stay beneath
    a roof
  That might be smote with judgment for the blas-
    phemies I said :
Would I jest at the Eternal, while His thunders rolled
    aloof,
  And His awful sword was flashing in the lightning
    overhead?

The world was blind and faithless, and full of vain
    conceit
  Of wisdom which was foolishness, and would not
    know the Lord ;
And I might write brisk words that, one day, I would
    fain delete
  When He came in his glory, whom the Universe
    adored.

I did not bid him stay, although the storm burst
    forth anew,
  And snapt a grand old pine as if it had been but
    a reed;
There were five behind our cottage, and I loved
    them, and I knew
  Their features and their voices, for they spoke to
    me, indeed.

They were like living things to me, with thoughts and memories
 And passions of the women in the untamed Druid times;
I heard them sing their skalds at night unto the raving seas,
 And moan their rugged lyke-wakes in the ancient Runic rhymes.

I called them Druid sisters, for I wist that they had seen
 The black priests in the forest, and the altars, and the smoke;
And in the evening still they talked to me of what had been
 Ere the Roman smote the savage, or the Christian morning broke.

Now, startled by the sudden crash, I did not think of him,
 But of the tall grey sister who was growing bald atop,
And grey with clinging lichen that had feathered every limb,
 And in my mind I saw her bow her lofty head, and drop,

While o'er their fallen sister all the others scream and moan
  In unrestrainëd anguish; so I did not bid him stay;
The night was wild and fearful, and the road was dark and lone,
  But he had the wild-beast instinct to surely find his way.

And so I let him go, and then I thought that I did right;
  Could any soul have sat there to be drenched with commonplace,
Slushed with dull ditch-water preachments, when the awe of that great night
  Had strung the mind to highest pitch, and touched the heart with grace?

My Being was at white heat, and he would have plunged it so,
  Hissing, into his cold water; and I did rebel at that;
And there are times when silence, if the preacher did but know,
  Shall preach to better purpose than a sermon stale and flat.

Thus he went forth in wrath, and I had no regretful thought
  Hearing him bang the door, and stride into the stormy night;
I sat in silence, ordering all the pictures I had got,
  Or glancing now at Hilda through the glimmering candle light.

By-and-by, the storm abated, and the moon came forth, at length,
  In a clear breadth of heaven, with all the countless host of stars,
And nature did assert the calm tranquillity of strength,
  And bridled with the Pleiades the wrath of angry Mars.

I looked out from my window to Orion and his belt;
  She looked out from her window to the lone star near the Pole;
And not a word we spake as yet, but in my heart I felt
  A shadow creeping coldly, like eclipse, across my soul.

There she sat, pale and anxious, with a wistful
    frightened look
  That seemed to shrink from me, although she
    neither spoke nor stirred;
There I sat, dull and listless, with my eyes upon
    a book
  Whereof, although I read and read, I knew not
    e'er a word.

Very silent were we both; but how I yearned for
    her I loved!
  As gazing through the candle-light, I saw her
    quivering lip,
And how the great tears gathered, and how the
    loose ring moved,
  Unconscious, from the knuckle to the slender
    finger-tip.

I thought I had done right; but I was not so sure
    next day;—
  Morning thoughts are sweet and tender—and I
    whispered my regret;
I had been vexed and angry; and I might have
    bid him stay;
  But hinted that his head would be the cooler for
    the wet.

Ah me! ah me! that thoughtless itch for saying
    clever things!
  Ah me! ah me! that little sense of what a word
    may do!
Ah me! the woeful echo from the weary past that
    rings
  Words that are very old now, but the grief is
    always new!

That day was full of rumours sad, of boats swamped
    out at sea,
  Guns booming in the offing, and wrecks strewn
    along the shore,
And the fierce-rushing river had flooded all the lea,
  And left but stones and gravel where the clover
    grew before.

Weary and sad, at evening I hasted home, with
    all
  My budget of ill news, to find yet worse awaiting
    there,
For Hilda, with a face that did my very heart
    appal,
  Sat, white and chill, beside the fire, with fixed
    and stony stare.

A fixed and stony stare at me! I think she knew
    me not,
  But shivered when I spoke, and seemed to shrink
    from me in dread;
And but for that long shudder my unwelcome
    presence brought,
  I hardly could have known if she were living then
    or dead.

O misery! to think the only sign of life should be
  A chill and shrinking quiver at the tender words
    I spake!
What was it? what had done it? who will tell the
    truth to me?
  And now I thought my head would reel, and
    now my heart would break.

But bit by bit, I gathered that she had gone out at
    noon
  To walk across the moor, and see the shepherd's
    sickly wife,
And nurse her sickly babe a while, and sing a
    quiet tune
  To still its ceaseless wailing, for it had faint hold
    of life.

And what she saw, or what she heard, or what had touched her wits,
  Our handmaid wist not, only she came home so ghastly pale,
And spoke not any word to her, but fell in swooning fits,
  And then sat with a stony look, or wailed a piteous wail.

Just then I heard a trampling and a shuffling at the door,
  And men came in thereafter with heavy, clumsy tread,
And laid a wet, lank burden there beside me on the floor,
  And every face that looked at me was ghastly as the dead.

They had been going home, and turned to look at the old pine
  Thunder-blasted in the tempest, when they saw him lying there;
Poor Luke! he was a godly man, and eloquent divine,
  And also shod the horses well, and acted just and fair!

So clumsily they told the tale, low-speaking, sad at
    heart,
  Losing a faithful friend in days of weary grief and
    care;
And now the truth flashed on me as I looked, and
    saw a part
  Of his hard features through the fell of moist
    and matted hair.

Scarce had he left my door, or but a score of paces
    gone,
  That evening, when a sudden fate had laid him
    with the tree,
And Hilda, coming home, had seen the dead man
    lying lone
  Among the pools of water, with reproach of her
    and me.

And that had driven her from her wits, and now
    she sat and stared,
  And shivered when I spake to her, and was dis-
    traught and wild;
And as I held her hand, and prayed, I vowed,
    too, that I shared
  Her sorrow and her faith and hope, and would
    be as a child.

Yea, I would be a child of God, if she would only look,
  I would believe whate'er she said, if she would only speak,
I would not care for fame or power, for glory or for book,
  If she would only kiss me with the kiss that I did seek.

A weary, woeful night it was, unbroken night to her,
  Through all the dismal hours, and O the anguish unto me!
But with the morning light, the day began to faintly stir
  With faint gleams of returning thought as lights upon the sea.

But from that day we were estranged: she spoke no word of blame,
  Or only blamed herself, but she was silent and apart;
We never spake about him, and we never named his name,
  But yet his shadow coldly lay between me and her heart.

It was as if my fate had been to drive her God
    away,
  To part her from all emblems and helps of things
    Divine ;
And she must walk without me now along the narrow
    way,
  And she must make atonement for the guilt that
    had been mine.

BOOK FIFTH.

Rev. Elphinstone Bell, Priest.

ONLY the Church, with her compacted Creeds—
Clear thought that grew from faith and holy deeds,
Like dew distilled beneath the calm clear sky
By her whose life may droop, but cannot die—
Only the Church, with Sacrament and Priest,
And sacred Liturgy, and saintly Feast,
And great traditions, can our hope restore,
Or save this land that bleeds at every pore.
She, like a loving mother watching late
Through the dark night, may still avert its fate,
Tending each symptom, nursing with fond care
The sinking life, while any life is there,
And drawing down by prayer the needed grace
Till day-break smite upon the weary face.

For woe is me! this land of saints, once trod
By hallowed feet of martyr-sons of God,
Who from their cradle in the Hebrides,
Swaddled in mists, and rocked by stormy seas,
Drove out the heathen, threw their altars down,
And bore the cross until they gained the crown,
And plying agencies of peace and right,
Filled it with light, and made it love the light,
And Heaven, because it was so brave and true,
Gave it great trials, and high tasks to do,
That it might win great glory—now it lies,
Torn by schismatic sects, whose rival cries
Screech as the dismal owl, when light is gone,
Calls to the bittern in great Babylon.
It was the Church that in the age of Faith
And Miracle, when Prayer was its life-breath,
Moulded our civil life, and taught the arts,
Framed the just law, and filled the busy marts,
Drained the waste marshes, felled the forests vast,
Ploughed the long furrow, trimmed the bending mast,
Piled the tall minster towers, and reared the school
And stately college with its cloistered rule,
Quickening man's thought, and polishing his wit,
And garnering wisdom in the books she writ;
Yet meekly still her toilsome path she trod,
And gave the glory of it all to God.

But now we drive her from her tasks so dear;
Unblest the school, unblest the fruitful year,
Schismatic pride would first unchristianize
The life it vainly hopes to civilize,
Would cut the roots from which it grew so grand,
Part Church and State, and make an Atheist land.

And what the fruit of all that fierce Dissent
Scorning God's holy Church and Sacrament?
We call ourselves a Christian nation still,
Boast how our Sabbaths all the Churches fill,
How in the furrow lies the plough at rest,
And the beached boat heeds not the sea's request,
And how all Labour pauses at the call
To worship Him whose grace is all in all.
But do we cease from sin? or only stay
The wholesome work, yet not to praise or pray;
But to compound for wrong, and to abuse
God's patience, yawning in the weary pews?
Think of the drunkard's home, the mother's brat,
Memorial of the shame she grumbles at,
The artful trick adulterating food,
The balance false, the measure rarely good,
The cooked accounts that puzzle even the wise,
And swindle large by arithmetic lies,
The pasty cloth that stands nor sun nor rain,

The gritty bread, more sand than wholesome
    grain,
The edgeless tools, the ships that will not sail,
Insured to sink, and swamped without a gale.
Lo! we have liberty, but scanty law,
And mocking unbelief for reverent awe,
Loud boasts of power that snorting steam has
    given,
And lauds of science for the praise of heaven.
Woe's me! you shall not pace the village street
At evening for the brawling crowds you meet,
Or brazen women, leering as you pass
The steaming dram-shop with its glare of gas.
No voice of prayer is heard, no wailing psalm
Sobs, penitential, through the star-lit calm;
God's Word is cheap, and therefore little prized,
The World his worship gets, and sin goes undis-
    guised.

Wherefore, I say, the Church herself must gird
To her high task, by ancient ardour stirred.
Too long her Priests have lowered her claim to be
The Light of Life by which the world shall see;
Too long in faint, apologetic strain
The Church has spoken, fitly so in vain;
Too long her beauteous Service has been left

To slovenly haste and carelessness, bereft
Of all its antique grace, and rich device
Of sacerdotal robes for sacrifice,
Its fragrant incense, and its altar-lights,
Its ministry of comely Acolytes,
Its hallowed ritual fittingly intoned,
And its great Mystery lifted high, and throned,
In sacred symbol, for the Faith of all
Who bow the knee to Christ, and on him call.
'Tis meet that she who speaks in name of God,
And smites man's sin with words, as with a rod,
And bids the penitent in peace depart,
And calms the troubled, heals the bleeding heart,
Should have her glorious robes, and solemn speech,—
Symbols of power to pardon and to teach
With all divine authority, and tell
Vexed heart and mind, Be still, for all is well.

O for the days of Faith! when patient thought
Brooded on things of God, and questioned not!
When consecrated lives atoned for sin
By service that the grace of life might win.
They fed the poor, they watched the bed of pain,
Nursed the plague-stricken, soothed the fevered brain,

Chaunted by day and night the holy Hours,
And gave to humblest tasks the highest powers;
For lowly worship swelled to bliss complete,
When kings and nobles washed the pilgrims' feet.

So would we labour that the Church may be
Glorious again; and that the world may see
Embodied life divine, Incarnate Truth,
Rising anew in its immortal youth,
Doing the work of God that heals and saves,
Blessing our cradles and our lowly graves.
Not ours, indeed, to strip from life the fit
Shadow of God that grandly lies on it;
Not ours the garish, earthly light that leaves
No dread obscurities, no o'erhanging eaves
For souls to nestle in, and haply wing
From shade to sunshine forth, and sweetly sing.
Still high in awful Heaven our Faith would see
Mysterious Godhead, One and Trinity;
Incarnate Mystery too in mercy sent,
And offered still in mystic Sacrament.
So let the Church be true, in word and deed,
To her high Mission and her holy Creed,

Her glorious traditions, and her claim
To speak to man in God's eternal name,
With Psalm and Prayer, and Cross and lifted Host,
And Praise shall be to Father, Son, and Holy Ghost.

So preached the Preacher to us once; an Oxford scholar, young,
  With bare, thin face and sallow, bare and shallow too his mind;
A narrow spirit, with a pulpit rhetoric high-strung,
  Something flat and commonplace, but very telling of its kind.

Rounded periods, rarely natural—fit movements of the hand—
Tones liquid, but monotonous—ejaculations oft
To emphasise a commonplace—a manner gravely bland
  In private, but with women very winning, gracious, soft;

These had won the hearts of many, gathered crowds
   into his pews,
  Though he had little light to give, and none at
    all to me;
And weekly in the Kirk the pulpit thundered at his
   views,
  And at all who to the Woman, or the Beast
    might bow the knee.

A pretty Church-revival now sprang up, with dainty
   hymns
  Artistically sung, and prayers with high intoning
    read,
And holly-wreaths at Christmas about the cherubims
  That smiled with puffy cheeks beside the tablets
    of the dead.

There were candles on the altar, there was incense
   in the air,
  A Reredos, and a crucifix that towered up like a
    mast;
And with forty minutes' singing, and forty minutes'
   prayer,
  And twenty minutes' preaching, we were coming
    right at last.

'Then he needed a new organ, and we had a grand bazaar,
  And raffles winning money as you might at whist or pool;
And a lady-volunteer who carried on a pretty war
  With a choir of surpliced children badly trained at Sunday school.

'Twas not the simple worship of our homely Presbyters,
  Nor yet the stately worship of the custom Catholic,
But a modern imitation, smacking of the milliner's;
  Bran-new devotions fashioned on the model of antique.

To me it felt all hollow; but yet the youth had zeal,
  Played pastor very diligent, had he had aught to say,
Spent days among the sick, and by the fevered bed would kneel,
  And patter o'er his little book, and hurry on his way.

Hilda took to him amazingly, went to his daily prayers
  And school and district work, and now was rarely found at home;
Quoted his tinsel pretty words, was full of church affairs,
  And when I jested at him was as crisp to me as foam.

Day by day the church she haunted, quite forsook her parish kirk,
  Took to wearing dingy dresses, russet-brown or iron-grey,
Fasted often, made her life a weary penitential work,
  With all its natural brightness now put carefully away.

Scarce an hour but had its service of reading or of prayer,
  Scarce a day but was a saint's day, and her saints were very grim;
They frowned at every pleasure, and they smiled at every care,
  And still she spoke to me of God, and giving all for Him.

Keenly I felt that, all the more the priestling was obeyed,
  The lonelier life was growing, and we drifted more apart;
We had not any words, but something on her spirit preyed,
  And ever-widening waters seemed to sunder heart from heart.

He led her on a way divine which was not human too,
  And that, I wist, was not the way that Christ had walked of old;
And common, homely duty now a daily burden grew,
  And common life was trifling, and all earthly love was cold.

What was it? People told me he was verging toward Rome;
  But Roman or Genevan, mattered little unto me;
God had his little children out at nurse in many a home,
  Who laid their Bible on His lap, or Cross upon His knee.

That could never work this mischief; all the churches had their popes;
 And I cared not for Pope Calvin more than Pius; as for beads
And crucifix and censers and chasubles and copes,
 If she had a fancy for them, they were prettier things than creeds.

What was it, then, that chilled her into frosty silence now,
 As days went dimly by, without the wintriest gleam of mirth
To brighten up her wistful look, or clear the clouded brow?
 And wherefore did she sigh like one a-weary of the earth?

For all the house grew silent, and her laugh was never heard,
 That wont to ring so cheery, and she sang but doleful hymns
About the pilgrim's travail, and the comfort of His Word,
 And the home that is eternal, and the shining seraphims.

I comprehend now better what it was that preyed
  on her
  As she brooded in her loneliness, and yearned for
    higher love;
For her heart went upward, dreaming of that little
  visiter
  Whom God had taken from her arms into the
    heaven above.

She thought we were not worthy to rear the child
  of God,
  Our home-air was too worldly for so pure a soul
    to breathe,
And while she meekly bowed beneath the chastening
  of the rod,
  About the rod of sorrow she would twine a holy
    wreath.

Ever her heart was longing for the life that is
  not here,
  And love that death can never touch with
    withering of its bloom,
And for the tender blossom that she laid with awe
  and fear,
  Yet with absolute assurance, in its little grassy
    tomb.

Upward her daily musings soared in wonder, hope,
  and awe,
　The heavenward meditations of a heart that found
　　no rest,
Save in thought-reflected vision of the glory where
　she saw
　The children with the Father folded in among
　　the blest.

All this I learnt long after, when I read the secret
　Book
　Of her solitary musing, blurred with many a tearful
　　stain ;
I had thought her cold unto me when I saw her
　absent look,
　But her soul was longing for the lost that cometh
　　not again.

I also found the priest upon her tender scruples
　played,
　Eager to make a saint now of the mediæval
　　kind,
Inventing fresh atonements, as the restless heart
　betrayed
　Their failure in the cravings of the still remorseful
　　mind.

She was daily in his thoughts, and she was ever
    in his prayers;
  He watched her sickly thought with pride, and
    nursed the deep disease.
O the honour to his work, the rich reward of all
    his cares,
  To have the training of a saint in evil days like
    these!

But this I knew not at the time; and as I cast
    about
  For any likely reason this new sorrow to ex-
    plain,
And could not find it in my work, nor in my
    deepening doubt,
  There sprang up in my brooding heart a thought
    of bitter pain.

For calling up the former days which happily had
    flown,
  I paused at Winnie Urquhart, with her talent and
    conceit;
Hilda was jealous at the time, I saw it in her
    frown,
  And heard it in the tapping on the carpet of
    her feet.

Was this the shadow on our life? and could her
    love expire
  In fumes of jealous anger, and in self-tormenting
    thought?
Had she so little faith in me, and in the altar-
    fire
  Which I had tended like a charge that from the
    heavens I got?

My heart had never wandered for a moment from
    its place;
  My faith had been unshaken, and unshadowed for
    an hour;
But now a chill crept o'er my soul, a gloom came
    on my face,
  And my distrusted love became a deep distrustful
    power.

And thus the strangeness grew—a silent gulf between
    us twain,
  A wan, still water, drifting us yet more and more
    apart:
A life of wrested meanings, and of keen mis-
    taken pain,
  While each, with wistful longing, wondered at the
    other's heart.

Yet once I tried to draw her close again, for love is strong,
 And O my love yearned for her love, and O my heart was sore!
But cold love will not warm again; and now the nights were long,
 Like a stretch of barren sand upon the day's unhappy shore.

But one bright summer evening—all the sadder for its brightness—
 I sat in the green arbour looking to the sleepy town;
Slumbrous-sweet syringa-blossoms hung about me in their whiteness,
 And the summer in its glory bore the burden of its crown.

Sat the coney on its haunches 'mong the grey sand near its hole,
 Crouched the hare in the long furrow where the tenderest barley grew,
And I bade the living creatures loving welcome in my soul,
 For life was not so lonely with them frisking in my view.

A yellow bee was drumming in the fox-glove where
   it shewed
  A spire of purple-spotted bells upon the sunny
   brae,
And my heart went back a-dreaming far along the
   changeful road,
  Till thought passed into tears, and all the scene
   grew dim and grey.

O sad our withered hopes amid the flush of leaf
   and flower;
  Sad the winter of the spirit with the summer's
   wealth around;
And the weird feeling came again upon me in that
   hour,
  That life was but a shadow flitting dimly on the
   ground.

Shadowy joys, and shadowy sorrows! shadows all
   I felt and saw!
  The old sense of unreality came back on me
   again
I had dreamt, and I was waking, and the morning
   air was raw,
  Or perhaps I only dreamt that I was waking up
   to pain.

There was a fate upon me, and it drove me on and on,
  And I must "dree my weird," alas, whatever it might be;
Yet was I but a shadow among shadows sitting lone,
  And waiting for the doom that moaned around me like the sea.

Then Hilda came up softly, and softly sat her down;
  I knew that she was very pale, and very often sighed,
Although I looked away from her unto the sleepy town
  Expecting that sure fate which from afar I had descried.

'Twas all as if I knew before the thing that was to be;
  'Twould not have startled me to hear that I must die that night!
Yet 'twas as if a shadow of no moment unto me,
  A fate and yet a dream—and very strange, yet very right.

In silence and constraint we sat, a short while, side
    by side,
  While leaf by leaf she plucked the flower in
    pieces at her waist
With thin and trembling hand; and with mechanic
    foot I traced
  Senseless scores upon the gravel, to be speedily
    effaced.

"I would do right," she said, "and yet I know not
    what to think,
  For things are not the same now as they used
    to be before;
And from the cross appointed us we may not dare
    to shrink,
  Nor close the ear to Him who standeth knocking
    at the door."

I knew this was her woman's way of drawing near
    to me,
  A hint that, like a bud, a little sunshine would
    unfold,—
A feeling out for any touch of answering sympathy,
  That all the burdened secret of her trouble
    might be told.

And O I should have let my heart flow freely out
    to hers,
  I should have met her longing, and mingled it
    with mine,
I should have wooed her o'er again, pleading with
    all that stirs
  The woman and the human, till she felt it was
    divine.

But I was never ready yet, was always wise too
    late;
  Right words come swiftly to my pen, but slowly
    to my lips;
And there was that Greek-feeling of the coming on
    of Fate,
  Which dulled me with its shadow like the gloom
    of an eclipse.

And under all there lay the petulant, brooding sense
    of wrong,
  The thought her jealous love distrusted mine, that
    trusted all,
And had been true to her as is the music to the
    song
  That subtlely links its movement unto every rise
    and fall.

Then, something seemed to break in me. I thought
    I heard it snap,
  Like string of lute or viol, and I did not seem
    to care;
There was no more to win or lose; my life had
    lost its sap,
  And shook but leafless branches creaking in the
    wintry air.

I scarce know what I answered, but it had no
    touch of grace;—
  'Twas something about making crosses where no
    cross was meant;
The anguish and the deadness drove me into
    commonplace,
  And the commonplace fell on her like a heart-
    less argument.

And still I see the great blue eyes, strange-gleam-
    ing like a ghost,
  From out of her pale face, as she made answer
    with a moan;
"At least, I shall not have to pay the price I
    dreaded most;
  God's love will break no human heart, unless it
    break my own."

She had brought to me her burden, and she brought
 it all in vain;
  O cursed conceit of being right which kills all
   noble feeling!
A little word of kindness would have saved a load
 of pain,
  A little word of love had wrought a miracle of
   healing.

She meant to tell me all her grief, and all her
 young heart's care,
  And all the fond atonements she was minded
   then to try;
She meant to seek my counsel for the purpose
 that she bare,
  On a scrupulous, troubled conscience that was
   sorely vexed thereby.

And I,—I had not heard her; but with blankest
 commonplace
  Had turned away from eager eyes that pleaded
   as for life,
Had spoken in tones of iron, with an unmoved iron
 face,
  And every word a cruel stab as with a cruel
   knife.

Now both again were silent; then she sighed, and
    went away,
  And by and by I rose, and passed down to the
    moaning sea,
Until the moon arose, and spread long tresses on
    the bay,
  And silent stars, with sad rebuke, seemed looking down on me.

Next day, I watched her going, calm, about her
    household work,
  Putting everything in order, sorting all with bated
    breath,
Desk and drawer, and banded letter; and her face
    was like a mask,
  While she put all in its place, as one prepares
    for coming death.

I could not but remember how, when that hope
    made us glad,
  Which ended in a little grave in the dim land
    of peace,
She, hoping not for motherhood, had tidied all she
    had,
  And writ out full directions for the time of her
    release.

They say, the strange new life that throbs beneath
    a mother's heart
  Feels often liker death ; I cannot tell ; but when
    I came
By chance, then, on the sorted drawers, and under-
    stood, in part,
  Their meaning, O the anguish, and the fear, and
    sense of blame !

And now again she hung above her boxes all the
    day,
  And went about the house, too, with a look pre-
    meditate,
Silent, counting all the linens, putting things in
    drawers away,
  And by the less disorder making home more
    desolate.

Books were gathered from the tables, and shelved
    in order due,
  Things that crowded on the mantelpiece were laid
    aside in drawers,
Familiar, old disorder now took shape as neat and
    new,
  And there was bundling of receipts, and labelling
    of jars.

She wrote out for our maid some thoughtful counsel for the days
  When I should be alone, and where to find what I might need,
And what my special likings were, and what my common ways,
  And ended with a prayer that heaven might bless her in her deed.

I knew not this till after; and I could not then divine
  The meaning of the order, and the look of rooms to let,
The packed and sorted linens, neatly marked with numbers fine,
  And careful noting of accounts, and clearing of her debts.

Only the days went by, as haunted by a coming Fate,
  That well I knew was closing on me, like the darkling night,
Till reaching home one evening, I found no loving mate
  Fluttering around our little nest amid the waning light.

Instead, there was a letter on the mantelpiece, that leant
　Against the marble clock—a blotted letter, sealed with black;
I did not need to read it then, to find out what it meant,
　As I saw the tremulous letters, faintly scrawled upon the back.

And yet it stunned me for a while; I held it in my hand,
　Staring at the superscription, though I wist not what I saw;
I know I locked the door too; for my sorrow could not stand
　The gaze of the scared housemaid, half in pity, half in awe.

Alone! my soul would be alone! it was a lonely lot
　That henceforth must be mine; but now I wanted solitude;
Like wounded deer that leaves the herd for some secluded spot
　To die in, so I shut me in, and felt that it was good.

I broke the seal, and read I knew not what, but
    all the night
  I paced in silent anguish up and down the silent
    room,
Now longing that the darkness might never see the
    light,
  Now praying for the light to scare the horror of
    the gloom.

I have it still, that letter—it is brown and tattered
    now,
  Often read, although its every word is burnt
    into my brain;
And well where every falling tear had blotted it I
    know,
  And every blot is in my heart a scar and aching
    pain.

THE LETTER.

Husband and Dearest, be not wroth with me,
Because I leave you for a little while.—
Only a little—one day to return,
A better wife, and make a brighter home,
For therefore do I go, with breaking heart;
And secretly, for it would break your heart

To let me go; and yet I needs must go,
That worse may not befall, and we, the more
We rub together, be but more estranged.

Often I thought to tell you all the thought
That brooded in me. But you did not care
To speak of what might grow into debate;
And I was fearful, knowing you have much
Upon your mind, and that it is not well
To fret the current of your larger thought
With small obstructions. What I mean is this;
Indeed, I did not mean to hide from you
My purpose, or to purpose anything
Unworthy; for wherever I may be,
My wifely heart goes with me, and the troth
I vowed to you; and that you know right well

But things are no more as they were with us;
Somehow the light has gone out from our life,
And we, together living, live apart
In joyless solitude. I blame you not,
Except that your too tender cherishing
Fostered my self-love, making much of me,
Petting myself, and pitying myself
Too much already. Mine alone the blame
Of that dim separateness. For I was not

The wife you needed, though I tried to be,
And never woman's love was more than mine.
I have not shared the burden of your thoughts,
I have not understood you, nor forgot
Myself in your high purpose; my small lamp
That feebly glimmered, failed, of course, to light
The too large chambers of your life. Perhaps,
I never should have been a wedded wife;
Perhaps it had been better had I died
When God took baby from us. I have been
Foolish and fretful, selfish, useless; only
I loved so absolute—that is my excuse.

Had I but loved my God as well! But there,
The more I strove that you should cleave to Him,
The more I seemed to lose my hold of Him,
And drifted as you drifted, helping not
Your soul, and hurting mine own faith, as day
Slipt after day, with ever dimmer sense
Of things unseen in me, and harder thoughts
In you, until I felt my darkening way
Was darkening yours, and dropping into death
As we more alien grew in all our thoughts,
In feeling more estranged, in ways more sundered,
And God appeared the further from us both.
That is the bitter end of all my striving—

Harm to my own soul, cruel hurt to thine!
And yet I meant so well; only I tried
A work beyond my power; except the Lord,
Do build the house, the builder builds in vain.

Bear with me; I am full of self-reproach,
As well I may be, and I must atone
For that so fruitless past, ere peace will come.
I have shunned sorrow, comforting myself
Till I have lost all comfort in myself;
And now I must seek sorrow for a while,
And wear the crown of thorns, and bear the cross.
And find a new life in them. Do not try
To hinder that on which my heart is set,
Which will redeem my life from shallowness,
And make its homely service, by and by,
Truer and purer; both to thee more helpful,
And happier to myself, forgetting self.
A little while—and then I shall come back,
Wiser by lessons gathered where the shades
Of the Eternal fold around man's life,
Saying, Be still, and know that I am God.
A little while—and but a little while,
Not long enough for either to forget,
Yet long enough for you to look beyond,
And find the fountain of a surer peace

Than ever I could give. A little while,
And we shall wed again, and make a home,
Where Christ will dwell with us, as we recall
This break as our true marriage.

        Farewell, now;
'Tis hard to write, and could not have been spoken;
And yet it must be : farewell, my beloved.
I have gone over all the house, and left
Some tears in every room, and take with me
Its picture in my heart. I think that all
Is left in order; if there's aught forgotten,
Forgive me, for my heart was very heavy.

I know you'll not forget to plant fresh flowers
Around the little grave. 'Tis nothing; yet,
When I return, I would not like to see
Another picture than I bear with me.

You cannot doubt the love I bear to you.
You cannot doubt the grief that weeps for you,
You cannot doubt the purpose that for you
Would school my heart by earnest discipline;
You cannot doubt me, even in leaving you
A little while, and but a little while,
For surely God will spare me unto you.

As I read that blotted letter, with its love so fond
    and true,
  Again in the dim morning, I was stung with
    new regret;
Why had I mooned away the night, when there
    was that to do
  Which still might heal our sorrow, and restore
    my darling yet?

O misery! O misery! to have been rich indeed,
  And to have wasted all that wealth of love by
    cold distrust!
And what were I without her, but a shivering,
    withered reed
  With the glad water at its roots all gone to
    summer dust?

I did not wish a wiser wife — I only wanted
    her?
  How could she think I cared for bookish women
    or their praise?
If she only saw my heart, and only felt the stir
  Of pain and shame and self-contempt I had for
    all my ways!

I hurried to our priestling; I was sure he had to do
  With this fresh sorrow of my life; and I misjudged him not;
He was fain to make atonement where atonement was not due,
  And manufactured crosses when Providence forgot.

I found him high and haughty in a saintly kind of way,
  But he allowed that she had joined a pious sisterhood
Who from a distant harbour would be sailing on that day,
  To nurse the wounded in the war, and do the dying good.

I waited not for more; 'twas idle to dispute with him:
  He had the true ascetic heart that knows no tie, or care
Of wife or child or kindred, and was fain to sing a hymn
  For "those in peril on the sea" when I was fain to swear.

O that journey to the seaport! O the thoughts that surged on me!
  O the reasons I would urge! the triumph I must surely win!—
But the anchor had been weighed, the ship was dropping out to sea,
  And I only looked on crowded decks, and heard confused din.

I saw the ship sway o'er the bar, I saw the hurrying crowd,
  And the sailors sang light-hearted, and the landsmen gave a shout;
But song and shout were in my ear lamentings low or loud,
  And whether all were truth or dream, I could not well make out.

I rushed along the granite mole that stretched far out to sea,
  Where angry waves were howling loud, like hungry beasts of prey;
O cruel waves whose crashing drowned the cry that came from me!
  O mocking waves that heeded not, but bore my love away.

The rain came down in plashes, gusty, sputtering in my face,
  And little, gushing runlets flowed down by me to the sea;
I felt their chill, but recked not, and shivering for a space
  Sat on the dripping stones, and leant my face upon my knee.

What followed then I cannot tell, I cannot tell how long—
  Sounds that made my blood to tingle, laughter mingled with long sighs;
And now I was athirst, and now was choking in a throng,
  And ever one pale visage looked on me with yearning eyes.

O God forgive us, Hilda; and God be good to thee!
  O my cold, distrustful silence, it was not the better part!
And O what would I give to bring my love back from the sea
  Whose billows, ever breaking on me, break my very heart.

Where art thou? where, my darling? the noise of
    war is stilled,
  The wounded sun them at the doors, or cripple
    through the street;
I ask them of my darling, and they tell me who
    were killed,
  Of the soldiers in the trenches, or the sailors in
    the fleet.

They tell me of the sisters, but they never speak
    of her;
  There was a sister Bridget, whom they never
    name without
Rubbing a sleeve across the eye, and talking of the
    stir,
  When they broke out of the trenches to assail
    the great Redoubt.

I wait and ask, and wait in vain; she passed away
    from me;
  The last glimpse that I had was when the ship
    swayed o'er the bar;
And all the hope of love went down into the
    stormy sea,
  And never tidings came from it, or from the
    storm of war.

Epilogue.

A MIGHTY city of tented streets,
   And never a house of brick or stone,
And the pulse of the city throbs and beats
   As if in a fever burning on;
Nothing but tents in all the plain,
Nothing but bronzed and bearded men,
With clashing sabre and jingling spur,
Plume of feather, or crest of fur.

Here are banners, and there are flags;
   All of their bravery now is stained;
As the wind flutters their tattered rags,
   Lo! where the powder and blood are grained
And the heavy air has a fœtid breath:
Is it of blood? or is it of death?
How the wild dogs and the birds are fat,
Gorged, where they lazily perch or squat!

EPILOGUE.

Now, at a tent-door steeds are champing,
    Now they are galloping forth with speed;
Down the long streets there are companies tramping,
    Grimly silent, on some fell deed;
Some in the wine-shop are drinking hard,
Some are gaming with dice and card;
Many a jolly stave trowls from those,
But these are coming to oaths and blows.

Hark! to the call of the bugle horn,
    Or the quick rattle of mustering drum!
Swift to the summons, at even or morn,
    Bronzed and bearded, the gallants come.
Balls from the rifle-pits *ping* about,
Great guns boom from the big Redoubt,
And the angry hiss of the burning shell
Screams through the fire and smoke of hell.

Far on the outskirts stands a tent,
    And over the tent a great red Cross;
Balls lie round, but their force was spent
    Long ere they rolled o'er the silent moss;
A cross is over the silent gate,
A cross on the arm of them that wait,
Emblem of pity and healing and peace,
Bidding the wrath of war here to cease.

One comes out of it, grave and sad;
   Just a whisper, and then returns;
What are the tidings now? good or bad?
   Still she lives, but the fever burns.
Then again silence reigns all about,
And the twilight pales, and a star comes out,
But yet the air seems to pulse and to throb,
Now and again, with a stifled sob.

Sudden, the sob is turned to a wail;
   What is it? where is it? Hush! the door
Opens again now, and all hearts fail;—
   He too is weeping, for all is o'er.
It is not night, and it is not day;
Calm in the twilight she passed away,
Just as the star, where the cloud was riven,
Pointed her way through the opening heaven.

Near the tent-door was a sickly group,
   And O the tears ran down their cheeks like rain;
One said, "There is not a man in our troop
   But would have died just to save her a pain:
I would have died for her; so would a score of us;
Broken and maimed, she was worth many more of us;
God help the poor fellows, now she is gone;
She was like my mother when last I was down."

When it was told at the drinking bar,
  The flagon untasted was dashed on the board;
Hushed was the chorus of glory and war—
  Others were trusted, but she was adored.
No one shuffled the cards again,
Rattled the dice now, or called a main.
"Who's for the trenches? we must have it out;
Now is the time, lads, to try the Redoubt."

Belted with hell-fire, and shrouded with smoke,
  Girdled with rifle-balls as with a wall,
Yet with a yell from the trenches they broke,
  Plunging through rifle-balls, hell-fire, and all.
'Twas not for glory they stormed the Redoubt;
'Twas that the grief of their wild hearts must out.
That was her monument; and they cried
"God and saint Bridget!" as each man died.

L'Envoi.

I DO but paint a picture, just to show
   How cracks the old crust of Faith beneath our feet,
   Partly by light from heaven and fervent heat,
Partly by fierce upheaval from below.

Here fissures deep are gashed; there but a rent
   Scores the shrunk surface thirsting for fresh showers
   To water its dry herbs and drooping flowers;
But everywhere is great bewilderment.

God's ploughshare trenches well, nor will He wait,
   And see His fallow lying all unbroke,
   Because another's heifer takes the yoke,
Nor is His furrow always clean and straight,

But still He maketh ready for His sowing,
    And scatters with the sweep of unseen hand
    Fresh seed of life upon the fresh-turned land,
And gathers cloud and sunshine for its growing.

O weep ye for the Home whose tottering wall
    The trembling heart with unfeigned anguish saw,
    And with untempered mortar daubed its flaw,
Faith lacking Faith that God is over all.

Weep, yet rejoice! for her unselfish deeds,
    Mightier than words, have bidden doubt away,
    And led him into light of better day,
And Love, which is the soul of all the Creeds.

WORKS
PUBLISHED BY MR. MACLEHOSE,
PUBLISHER TO THE UNIVERSITY, GLASGOW.

Second Edition, in Extra Fcap. 8vo, Price 6s. 6d., Cloth.

OLRIG GRANGE:

A Poem in Six Books.   Edited by HERMANN KUNST, Philol. Professor.

Examiner.

"This remarkable poem will at once give its anonymous author a high place among contemporary English poets, and it ought to exercise a potent and beneficial influence on the political opinions of the cultivated classes. . . . The demoralizing influence of our existing aristocratic institutions on the most gifted and noblest members of the aristocracy, has never been so subtly and so powerfully delineated as in 'Olrig Grange.'"

Pall Mall Gazette.

"'Olrig Grange,' whether the work of a raw or of a ripe versifier, is plainly the work of a ripe and not a raw student of life and nature. . . . It has dramatic power of a quite uncommon class; satirical and humorous observation of a class still higher; and, finally, a very pure and healthy, if perhaps a little too scornful, moral atmosphere. . . . The most sickening phase of our civilization has scarcely been exposed with a surer and quieter point, even by Thackeray himself, than in this advice of a fashionable and religious mother to her daughter."

Spectator.

"The story itself is very simple, but it is told in powerful and suggestive verse. The composition is instinct with quick and passionate feeling, to a degree that attests the truly poetic nature of the man who produced it. It exhibits much more of genuine thought, of various knowledge, of regulated and exquisite sensibility. The author exhibits a fine and firm discrimination of character, a glowing and abundant fancy, a subtle eye to read the symbolism of nature, and great wealth and mastery of language, and he has employed it for worthy purposes."

Daily Review.

"A remarkable poem,—a nineteenth century poem,—the work of a genuine poet, whoever he may be, and of a consummate artist. . . The story is wrought out with exquisite beauty of language, and a wealth of imagery which mark the writer as one full of true poetic sensibility, and keenly alive to all the subtle influences that are at work in society."

Academy.

"The pious self-pity of the worldly mother, and the despair of the worldly daughter are really brilliantly put. . . . The story is worked out with quite uncommon power."

English Independent.

"There is a music in portions of the verse which is all but perfect; while for vigorous outline of description, raciness and pungency of phrase, and condensation of thought, we know no modern volume of poems that is its equal. . . . The satire is most searching, the pathos tenderness itself, and once or twice the passion becomes almost tragic in its intensity. From the first page to the last the fascination is fully maintained."

WORKS PUBLISHED BY MR. MACLEHOSE.

Second Edition, Extra Fcap. 8vo, Cloth, Price 7s.
BORLAND HALL,
A Poem in Six Books. By the AUTHOR of 'OLRIG GRANGE.'

Scotsman.

"The publication of another work by the author of 'Olrig Grange' may be described as a literary event of no small importance. In almost all essential points 'Borland Hall' marks an advance on the powers exhibited in 'Olrig Grange.' The remarkable rhythmic resource displayed in that book is more richly illustrated here. There is still more of dramatic force in the construction of the story, in the conception and contrast of character; and at least an equal degree of knowledge of human nature. The ease and felicity of expression which made it difficult to believe that 'Olrig Grange' was not the work of a practised hand are just as conspicuous in 'Borland Hall,' and a strong yet subtle humour here also asserts itself as one of the author's chief characteristics. Beyond all this he displays a wealth of lyric power which is in itself a better stock-in-trade, so to say, than many a successful poet possesses. Songs of exquisite beauty stud the poem like gems in some massy work of beaten gold. . . . There are many charming little lyrics scattered through the book which deserve close reading. We must content ourselves with repeating that 'Borland Hall' is a book in which original and vigorous thought, rare dramatic instinct, and profound knowledge of human nature are embodied in poetry of a very high class. We do not claim for the author the rugged strength or the broad and deep genius of Browning, nor can it be said that he stands, in regard of mastery of rhythm and exquisite grace of language, on a level with Tennyson. But he possesses in a very large degree the distinctive qualities of both these great poets; and his latest work is not only notable in itself, but full of splendid promise."

Glasgow News.

"The appearance of a new poem by the author of 'Olrig Grange' is an event of some importance in the literary world. His former work at once gave its writer a lofty standing among contemporary British poets. The author did not climb to fame by laborious steps and slow, but sprang at a bound into a position such as only genius can attain. . . . 'Olrig Grange' was altogether such a success as it is given to few poems to achieve; and when it became known that the author was engaged on a second work, expectation ran high. Poets who have made their mark on their first venture may well be nervous when they essay a second—it is so hard to go on excelling, and to come up to the higher standard by which each successive effort is sure to be judged. In 'Borland Hall,' however, the author of 'Olrig Grange' has overcome the difficulty we have mentioned. He has not only come up to, but gone beyond the expectation raised by the earlier poem. 'Borland Hall' surpasses 'Olrig Grange' both in power and finish. It conveys the idea that the author has acquired a greater mastery over his art without sacrificing in the least any of his originality and vigour. There are still some roughnesses, but they have such a quaint, racy flavour, that we would not dispense with them if we could. . . . 'Borland Hall' is a book to be read. It is the matured fruit of the poetic inspiration which produced 'Olrig Grange.' The sweep of the poet's fingers on the strings of his lyre are firmer and stronger. He has come to know his power, and to use it with confidence. There is nothing weak in the book—no sickly sentimentality, no flavour of the 'poesy' of the drawing-room. Every line is stamped with the strength of vigorous manhood."

www.ingramcontent.com/pod-product-compliance
Lightning Source LLC
Chambersburg PA
CBHW021344230426

43666CB00006B/399